Sugar Daddy Capitalism

Sugar Daddy Capitalism

The Dark Side of the New Economy

Peter Fleming

polity

First published in 2019 by Polity Press

Polity Press
65 Bridge Street
Cambridge CB2 1UR, UK

Polity Press
101 Station Landing
Suite 300
Medford, MA 02155, USA

ISBN-13: 978-1-5095-2819-6
ISBN-13: 978-1-5095-2820-2 (pb)

A catalogue record for this book is available from the British Library.

Typeset in 10 on 16.5pt Utopia Std by Servis Filmsetting Ltd, Stockport, Cheshire
Printed and bound in Great Britain by CPI Group (UK) Ltd, Croydon

The publisher has used its best endeavours to ensure that the URLs for external websites referred to in this book are correct and active at the time of going to press. However, the publisher has no responsibility for the websites and can make no guarantee that a site will remain live or that the content is or will remain appropriate.

Every effort has been made to trace all copyright holders, but if any have been overlooked the publisher will be pleased to include any necessary credits in any subsequent reprint or edition.

For further information on Polity, visit our website: politybooks.com

Contents

Introduction

The Economics of Sleaze

In October 2017, Hollywood mogul Harvey Weinstein was embroiled in a remarkable scandal that would have far-reaching consequences. It was alleged that for many years he'd abused his considerable power by sexually harassing and assaulting young women.[1] After the first accusation hit the headlines, other women stepped forward. It wasn't just aspiring actresses who had fallen prey to his lechery, but employees in his own company too.[2] In subsequent weeks the scandal would significantly widen, with iconic actors and directors accused of similar behaviour.

Most focused on Weinstein's louche character, casting the issue in strictly moral terms. Other commentators, however, suggested we place his predation in an economic context, one that is conducive of such behaviour.[3] A trade union official pointed out that the situation faced by Weinstein's staff is typical of that in many jobs today: 'think about a young woman doing bar work, or working in hotels; all those kind of jobs where you can be replaced overnight if you don't play along'.[4] Vulnerable women were easy targets for Weinstein because the economic penalties they'd incur for rejecting his sexual advances were clear.[5] Weinstein had other ways to keep people quiet. His company insisted employees sign non-disclosure agreements.[6] And when his victims threatened to go public, he hired corporate-intelligence agents – including ex-Mossad spies – to besmirch their reputations.[7]

Regardless, it didn't take long for the world to find out what was going on. The most creepy revelation was about Weinstein's notorious 'business meetings'. He would have an assistant invite young women to a hotel bar on the pretence of a job opportunity. Soon they'd be in his private room. Finally Weinstein would be standing there in a bathrobe demanding a massage. One victim recalls her business meeting with the film producer. The description is interesting because it foregrounds the complex entanglement of career advancement, sleaze and power:

> I, too, went to the meeting thinking that perhaps my entire life was about to change for the better. I, too, was asked to meet him in a hotel bar. I, too, met a young, female assistant there who said the meeting had been moved upstairs to his suite because he was a very busy man. I, too, felt my guard go up but was calmed by the presence of another woman my age beside me. I, too, felt terror in the pit of my stomach when that young woman left the room and I was suddenly alone with him. I, too, was asked if I wanted a massage, champagne, strawberries. I, too, sat in that chair paralyzed by mounting fear when he suggested we shower together. *What could I do? How not to offend this man, this gatekeeper, who could anoint or destroy me?*[8]

The scandal soon rocked other institutions far away from Hollywood, including the Houses of Parliament in London, as women told their own stories during the '#Me Too' campaign.[9] A culture of sexual harassment at Parliament Buildings had allegedly been festering for years and was now out of control. It was revealed that one MP even had a young assistant (whom he called 'sugar tits') purchase sex toys for his mistress.[10] A specific employment arrangement prevailed here

2

too. Westminster assistants 'are effectively self-employed' and thus on the nasty end of a very unequal power relationship.[11] They have few protections like those of regular workers and are basically on their own. Finally, there is what I call the neoliberal knockout punch in this regard: if workers don't like any of this, then no one's pointing a gun at their head. They're always free to leave.

Penis Captivus

This book is not really about sexual harassment. But these disturbing cases do help capture a broader shift in Western economies that I want to explore: namely, *deformalization*, whereby public officialdom and regulatory protection are absent in the business world. The deformalization of Western capitalism is a delayed and largely unanticipated outcome of the neoliberal revolution masterminded by neoclassical economists, particularly F. A. Hayek and Milton Friedman of the 'Chicago School'.

This loose group of scholars and academic activists didn't agree on all matters (Hayek challenged Friedman on monetary policy, for example). But they did share one dream. In an ideal society everyone would interact on a strictly private and personal basis. Money and self-interest would be the only universal principles permitted, with governments coming into the picture only as a last resort.[12] Hence their undivided love of capitalism.

Margaret Thatcher and Ronald Reagan were so bewitched by the Chicago School that they made it their life mission to liberate capitalism from the shackles of big government. Business can regulate itself; private-market individualism represents the ultimate pinnacle of personal freedom; we no longer need governmental standards, labour laws or unions; pay rates and contractual terms/conditions are a private matter, negotiated behind closed doors between individuals. As long as it's legal, anything goes. It is little wonder that Harvey Weinstein soon makes an appearance to exploit the grey zones of this new economic universe.

Informality isn't bad *per se*, of course. Some of the most progressive and spontaneously cooperative gestures have emerged outside the state and big business.[13] But I want to explore deformalization specifically in relation to market individualism. It's being disseminated everywhere. How exactly did the cool rationalization of daily life under neoliberal capitalism end up intersecting with a reliance on some all-too-human power relationships, many of which are frighteningly arbitrary and contingent in nature?

On the surface, the ideas promoted by the Chicago School seem distant from the murky and underhand world of Weinstein and his backroom deals. Hayek and Friedman believed that *capitalism unbarred* would lead to a fairer society because our lives would be shaped by: (a) individual merit on the one hand, and (b) cold cash objectivity on the other. The economy could finally be rid of partiality and bias because the price mechanism has little respect for tradition, family connections or personal history. Whether you're black or white isn't important – green is the only colour that counts. Neoliberal thinkers loved the idea. *Quantity* or 'how much?' ought to be the only bond connecting people, not *quality* or 'who are you?' Hayek had such faith in the notion that he declared money to be man's greatest invention for obtaining liberty.[14] If society was rebuilt around this tenet, then we'd all soon be rich micro-entrepreneurs, free to tailor our working lives to individual taste rather than be handcuffed to global standards imposed by trade unions and government.

This is all fantasy, of course. That's why reading Hayek's *The Road to Serfdom* or *The Constitution of Liberty* today is like encountering a work of fiction given how abstract its assumptions are.[15] There are no real people involved. This is particularly so regarding its strident individualism, which has always been a dubious part of the mythology of capitalism. Hayek pursues it *reductio ad absurdum* and no society can function that way. Moreover, we now know that capitalist economies can't do without the state, since so-called 'free trade' requires a thick rulebook and governmental protection for big business interests. Indeed, if a welfare state still exists, it's geared towards helping corporations rather than those most in need.

Dark Corners

Although Hayek and Friedman are no longer seriously studied in mainstream economics and often dismissed as relics of the Cold War, their legacy is still writ large almost everywhere in Western societies today – but not quite in the way they envisaged, which is my point. Reorganizing society to privilege financial individualism didn't depersonalize business and commerce as boldly predicted in *The Road to Serfdom*. In fact, the opposite seems to have occurred, with Weinstein and the British Houses of Parliament indicative examples. Why so? As the public sphere recedes and the private sector grows to fill the gaps, trusted to regulate itself, the cash nexus certainly reigns supreme *à la* the Chicago School, but simultaneously takes on some very informal characteristics. Here, both questions of quantity ('how much?') and quality ('who are you?') inform economic life. That's mainly because the formalistic backdrop of legal protections and labour standards is not supposed to feature much in this new economic order.

This might be great if you are rich. But if you're not, then trouble soon looms. The isolated individual inevitably finds themselves in an insurmountable power struggle where all kinds of demands can be made of them because their bargaining leverage is limited. It's not hard to see why some bosses might take advantage of this, not only in the seedy way that Harvey Weinstein did, but in terms of economic exploitation too or what might be called *flexploitation* in the age of Uber-jobs. Positive informality – where close colleagues might help each other out, working around a pointless rule – is replaced by an *inverse personalism*, where the cold logic of economic rationality is delivered in the embodied form of a sleazy boss or sadistic customer.

This brutal personalization of labour – where there are no pooled or social goods in terms of sharing the costs and benefits of work – severely delimits our societal potential. In fact, it's probably making us stupider, not to mention more insecure and desperate. Recent research has discovered that our creative and cognitive abilities are super-boosted when situated in a public or shared domain. For example, psychologists Dan Sperber and Hugo Mercier discuss an experiment in which a classroom of people are asked to solve a tricky word puzzle.[16] In the first version, everyone worked in isolation. Only two participants came up with the correct answer. In the second variation, people were encouraged to debate and discuss the puzzle. When they sat down and did the test, a much higher percentage was successful. What was in fact an instance of *public reason* raised the game of the entire classroom, and I think the same applies to economies too – in terms not only of productivity but also of civility, particularly in those institutions where democratic dialogue is least welcome, such as the modern workplace.

What makes neoliberal capitalism especially troublesome in its current form is the way it overlays this individual isolation with economic anxiety, a mood that begins to structure the very web of everyday life. Apprehension itself is now financialized. Scientists have discovered that scarcity – either real or perceived – keeps us fixated on very short-term challenges (i.e., paying the next bill, applying for the next job, etc.). Over time, this dims our universal reasoning abilities and effectively handicaps us compared to those who don't have to worry about money.[17] The conclusion is clear. It's time to repossess economic reason as a public good, since the benefits are so patently obvious, even by capitalism's own standards *apropos* innovation, creative thinking and growth.

Ghost Jobs

A central concern for critics opposing neoliberal capitalism today is the soul-deadening depersonalization it engenders as money floods into every part of our lives. Bonds no longer matter. All is commodified and rendered superficial. Community spirit is wiped away in a grey wave of financialization. Non-transactional relationships are nearly impossible under such circumstances. The bulldozer of money strips our world of softness and authenticity. No wonder mental illness explodes in such environments.[18] Add computerization to the mix and things get very depressing according to Franco 'Bifo' Berardi, a brilliant critic on this topic. Digital slavery erases our unique biographies and replaces it with an endless stream of productive time: 'when we move into the sphere of infolabor, there is no longer a need to buy a person for eight hours a day indefinitely. Capital no longer recruits people, but buys packets of time, separated from their interchangeable and occasional bearers. Depersonalized time has become the real agent of valorization and depersonalized time has neither any right, nor any demand.'[19]

Concrete work still feels *real* in a bodily sense. High blood pressure and neurosis have become a normal part of the job, after all. But the process of labour also takes on some eerie, ghostly attributes, because (from capitalist's perspective) employees are not really *there* in any singular, bodily sense. They're merely interchangeable e-cogs in a global computer system, one that is painfully administrative and blind to who you really are.

This bleak diagnosis is correct. But the narrative misses the dialectical underside of cash depersonalization, the 'cult of the informal', where near-claustrophobic moments of human familiarity close in upon us. This is exemplified by the individualization of work and the spread of freelancing, on-demand part-time work and insecure jobs in the so-called 'gig economy'.[20] The impersonal price mechanism is paramount, of course. But as individuals become super-reliant on an employer (or landlord, etc.), informal connections and 'favours' come into the picture too. Now the boss no longer demands just your objective time, as measured in monetary units. He also wants your arse. Power relationships of the *ultra-personal* kind come to the fore, trading in a sort of 'negative sociality' that is constantly in your face. Conspicuously missing in this inverted *socius* are the abstractions that used to foster solidarity (class, community, etc.) against capitalism. The social imagination risks being emptied of all generalizations other than that of money.[21] This is now the kingdom of lone individualism.

In this context, we see three forms of labour defining the new economy. The *employee* represents traditional paid employment, involving a contract, regular hours and statutory rights. Next we have the *self-employed* (freelancers, contractors, etc.), who can legally be paid below minimum wage and have few of the rights of standard employees. They make up the growing army of Uber jobs. Then there's *workers*. They are frequently employed on a contingent and fluctuating basis, involving on-demand contracts, and can be terminated at will. However, this third category has become increasingly amorphous, comprising activities we might better term 'ghost jobs' that can even escape the formal category of paid employment altogether. The border between obtaining an income and daily life is difficult to discern. Take a young woman who joins a Sugar Daddy 'dating' site to meet older men for money. Is she a sex worker or not? It's hard to tell. This blurring of money and life is something Hayek and the Chicago School overtly championed, of course.[22] Only today it's being filtered through the matrix of corporate power and economic austerity. Living itself has become a crazy sort of factory. It's not surprising that Uber claim to be nothing more than a car-pooling app, helping ordinary citizens share a ride, seamlessly interconnected with things people would be doing anyway.[23]

Insecure jobs (part-time, on-demand, freelancing, contracting, etc.) still only make up a relatively minor part of the overall labour market in OECD countries, which looks to change soon given current trends.[24] However, my argument is not simply numerical (how many jobs can be categorized as such); it's the *tone* that this third type of labour sets for the workforce as a whole that is interesting. A recent UK study found, for example, that an oppressive sense of precarity has quietly descended over most occupations, regardless of whether they're in the gig economy or not. Around 70 per cent of workers are worried about their employment situation, as if they're breathing the same air as an overworked and stressed Deliveroo rider: 'economic insecurity now stretches right throughout our labour market, including within jobs that appear safe on the surface'.[25] Uberization therefore operates in an insidious fashion, not only by exploiting its immediate workforce, but also by casting millions of other jobs in a doubtful light. All of a sudden, hard-won rights look like questionable privileges – perhaps even frivolous to some employers.

The 2018 university pensions dispute in the UK is a good example of this. The conflict was mainly about employers seeking to shift the risk of the pension fund and its investments on to employees. If the fund fails, then it's your problem alone, representing a radical change in the employment contract. The draconian initiative wouldn't have seen the light of day if Uberization hadn't been at work in other sectors of the economy. A 'Hitler Downfall Parody' – in which new subtitles are inserted over the film's famous bunker scene, having the tyrant explode on topics ranging from Starbucks and Sarah Palin to Xbox Live – summed up the employers' attitude in the dispute perfectly. When informed about striking faculty, Hitler is livid: 'Pensions! They are lucky to be paid . . . who needs academics? It's a hobby for them, it's a way of life. They don't need pensions!!'

For this reason, any critical investigation of Sugar Daddy Capitalism can't limit itself to Lyft and TaskRabbit, since they're merely bolder realizations of an ideology that is currently reshaping many occupations. The ideology I'm referring to is neoclassical economics, of course. Uber's rather outrageous argument that it (technically) has no employees driving taxis might seem an eccentric one. But it's indicative of how mainstream economists view the workforce more generally. There's a long tradition in libertarian thought that effectively erases labour from the official narrative of industrial activity, referring to 'human capital' or 'price takers' instead[26] – anything but paid employees with shared interests and concerns of their own.[27]

It's in this ideational milieu that ghost labour gains a firm foothold. Work is first individualized and then blended into the fabric of human life. Formal divisions between you and the economy (e.g., work time versus private time, etc.) fade into an inscrutable social backdrop as a result. Personal responsibility and self-reliance are revered like gods. Hence there is a fundamental tension that underscores jobs and employment today. When labour is deleted on an abstract level – in econometric theorems or Lyft profit/loss statements – it is simultaneously reinstated in a very intimate, concrete way. Works ceases to be an *external* activity – amenable to wider sociological categories populated by others doing the same thing. No, your job is more about 'who' you are (and know) as an isolated individual, making it a very private affair that is technically never-ending.

Facebook . . . Hell?

This change in the texture of employment can be seen in Ilana Gershon's fascinating study of job-seekers in the USA.[28] In the cartoon version of neoliberalism, everything ought to be coolly transactional, impersonal and desocialized. But that's not the only thing Gershon found in her interviews. A closely curated presentation of self was considered essential as job seekers adopted a 'self-as-business' metaphor, treating themselves as a social brand. Like Coca-Cola or Microsoft, this human iBrand needs to be carefully managed in order to project attributes that employers find desirable. Gershon observed people cautiously correcting Facebook posts – thinking tactically about the extramural interests listed on their résumé, and so forth. In short, these job seekers were *selling themselves*, not just their objective skill set. This ends up making workers very dependent on an employer's personal judgement, however fickle and unpredictable it may be. What's more, the effort of self-selling doesn't obey the usual boundaries we once erected between personal time and being on the job. These individuals were *always* on the make, a permanent micro-enterprise, since their economic survival depended on it.

As Gershon's study indicates, the ideology of work has escaped the factory walls. The logic of production has now meshed with living as such. This is how deformalization fuels flexploitation because it's difficult to see how conventional employment laws apply. We're dealing with deregistered private individuals. Here Uberization also takes a major cue from Friedman's attack on occupational licensing and permits, something I will discuss later in the book. For him, professional certification – such as training six months to become a London black-cab driver – is an excuse for closing out other workers and thus keeping wages/prices artificially high.[29] In a properly functioning free market, Friedman averred, there should be no restrictions on who's permitted to enter an occupation, including medicine and law. Planning restrictions and local authority by-laws restrict enterprise in a similar fashion, according to this philosophy. A true entrepreneurial society simply lets businesses get on with things. Deliveroo is taking this nation of deformalization to a new level. It is going to open 200 'dark kitchens' across the UK, pop-up cooking facilities that track demand and can be located in obscure backstreets and alleys.[30] A debate is currently being had about the planning ordinances that normal restaurants must observe. Do they apply to dark kitchens?

Even money itself isn't immune to this deformalization process, as indicated with the rise of blockchain and alt-currencies such as Bitcoin, Litecoin, Monero and XRP (or Ripple), which use untraceable cryptography to ensure anonymity or pseudonymity at the point of exchange. Governments around the world are anxious about alt-currencies. The state relies on centralized monetary policy and regulation over money supply via Central Banks – this can only work if it enjoys a monopoly over issuing currency.[31] Could the state effectively manage interest rates if bitcoin became a dominant money form, for example? Cryptocurrencies may well represent a left-wing victory for local self-governance as some have argued, especially anarchists. But the idea also has roots in capitalist libertarianism, especially the Austrian variant. For Hayek and his mentor Ludwig von Mises, alt-currencies could effectively dethrone the state and its monopolistic control over economic management.[32]

States of Disgrace

The hatred of bureaucracy and its mindless conflation with 'big government' and 'state profligacy' has been a major driver of the deformalization movement. While the revolt against bureaucrats is also seen on the anti-capitalist left, it's the free-market libertarians who've truly made it their own, creating an ideological battering ram to dismantle the public sphere at almost every turn. Wealthy conservative politicians in the USA and UK announce that they're standing for the average citizen who's drowning in absurd 'red tape', whilst killing off the very public services this same citizen depends on. As a result, administrative vigilance has been seriously compromised where we need it most: food hygiene inspections, rental market controls, and so forth.[33] Three additional issues are noteworthy.

First, right-wing detractors of government in Western societies almost never mention its primary mission, namely the facilitation of open democracy and accountability. That's probably why they prefer the more anaemic phrase 'political process' instead, especially Chicago School economists like Gary Becker and James M. Buchanan – often with a hint of disdain. In the age of austerity, democracy is even blamed for the global mess the economy is in because public debt and inflation stem from politicians promising too much and irresponsibly seeking votes.[34] The attack on 'big bureaucracy' is probably more telling of the elite's distrust of democracy *per se*, encouraging the privatization of problems that are *systemic* in nature, many of which derive from the financial oligarchy. At any rate, a vibrant public sphere is essential to counter the troubling aspects of deformalization we shall soon be discussing. In other words, it's time to reclaim the state. But is it reclaimable?

Second, it is ironic that the private sector – so lauded by neoclassical economics for its entrepreneurial vim – is today where we really find a lot of bloated bureaucracies, many of which are monopolistic and anathema to any sort of innovation.[35] This is perceptively noted in David Graeber's book *The Utopia of Rules* and its forensic dissection of 'total bureaucracy'.[36] Missing in studies like this, however, is the informal sphere that has ironically burgeoned behind the scenes at the same time – something I link to the marketization of life as prescribed by Hayek and Friedman.

And third, although neoclassical economics nominally cherishes private individualism and a minimalist state, this isn't quite how many of us experience capitalism today. Rather than disappearing, the state has been reshaped into a punitive enforcer, essentially devoid of any public mission.[37] This depressing transformation has taken place over time. The Nanny State of the post-war period morphed into the more distant and aloof Stepmother State of the 1980s and 1990s. But, today, we have something closer to an abusive Daddy State.[38] Neoliberal governmentality displays a strange admixture of intrusive symbolic violence and reckless neglect, particularly towards workers. Sure, governments are happy to turn a blind eye to the dark side of Uber jobs and offshore tax havens that hide billions, as revealed recently with the leaked Paradise Papers. On a parallel register, however, the state has never been so busy in our daily lives. This is mainly in terms of surveillance and policing, especially if you don't have the money to purchase exemption. For most 99 percenters, perhaps the following motto sums up what the state means today: Yes, you're on your own . . . *but that doesn't mean you're left alone.*

Neoclassical economists and policy-makers still refuse to acknowledge this grim reality of pan-privatization, despite the mounting evidence before us. If the judgement of money is technically blind towards all involved – they continue to believe – it will tame the dogs of wanton prejudice. It's somewhat incredible that this libertarian hypothesis is still espoused, given the atrocious failures we've witnessed in the wake of the 2008 crash. In a recent speech defending Airbnb and the gig economy, for example, Chief Secretary to the UK Treasury Liz Truss robotically cited the ideas of Friedman and his entrepreneurial individual.[39] For Truss, 'gig economy firms like TaskRabbit and AirBnB have brought fresh possibilities to all kinds of people, including those who were previously left behind . . . Uber is particularly used by those on low incomes . . . I love living in a country where businesses and individuals can pursue their own dreams and desires with the minimum of interference.'

Still echoing the Chicago School after all these years, influential officials continue to insist that this is how the road to personal liberty is paved.[40] Freedom is an exclusively private business, no more than two people meeting to make a 'deal'.[41] This book suggests that another path can unfurl from this ideological universe, one leading to a dimly lit hotel room. Inside awaits an overweight man in a bathrobe. He's willing to help you get that lucky break . . . for a price.

Chapter One

Uberfamiliar

Over the last few years, a number of adverts on Craigslist and similar sites have illustrated the level of economic desperation people are facing in the long wake of the global financial crisis.[1] These 'rent-for-sex' listings appear in the accommodation section of the website, typically in cities experiencing rising income inequality, a massive housing shortage and a euthanatized public sphere. Here are some examples:

$1 seeking young female roommate- free stay (Denver)

I recently got out of a very long relationship. I want something very different. I'm looking for a young girl 18–20 who also wants something different. Maybe you are new here and need help. Or maybe you are getting out of a bad relationship and have nothing. Maybe no job or a shitty job you hate. Maybe you need place to stay, use of a car, new clothes, nice dinners, maybe travel (i love to go to Las Vegas for quick getways) etc.

Contact me and i will let you know what i am looking for in return . . .

£1 / 1br – Free single room in flat for Black Woman (London)

This is my fantasy. Lovely room available for a broadminded black lady for 6 months only. A chance for you to save some money as you pay no rent. I'm normal easygoing guy in his 40s.

My fantasy is that we live normally, giving you your own space & you let me lick your bumhole once a week. Serious replies with details of age, size & height with photos get first response.

Such rent-for-sex listings have proliferated and are a product of the times. In the dark neoliberal wasteland otherwise known as London, for example, the trend has become acute.[2] Successive governments left the task of building new accommodation to the free market, which failed miserably to keep up with demand.[3] Moreover, accommodation has suffered from an incredible speculation bubble, where faceless offshore firms (typically based in tax havens) see an easy investment opportunity, increasing rent for everyone else.[4] For this reason, the so-called 'shortage' of housing can perversely coexist in communities with a large number of empty properties. Couple this with low wages and a personal debt crisis, and it's no wonder some choose to sell their bodies in order to have somewhere to live.

The Age of Rent

Rent-for-sex is an extreme example of exploitation, of course. But it captures a broader mood among those struggling to live in a world that has been privatized to death. Here the market has been left to its own devices *à la* the prescriptions of neoclassical economics and the Chicago School. As a result, a predatory class of private rentiers have emerged. Because the options are so limited for people and they can easily find themselves homeless, tenants are frequently too afraid to complain about damp bedrooms or maltreatment from landlords.[5] They are at the mercy of the property owner, a scenario we'd expect in some pre-industrial era, rather than 2018.[6]

A report pinpoints the issue succinctly, identifying characteristics that have increasingly reshaped other institutions too, including work, education and so forth: 'it seems astonishing that the private rented sector . . . has no regulator, no ombudsman and no redress scheme . . . there are hundreds of thousands of landlords who have not had to pass a test of competence, demonstrate any knowledge of landlord or tenant law, or prove their honesty, financial probity . . . let alone have any experience of property management'.[7]

There's always been an informal economy, of course. In poorer countries, global deregulation has seen this sphere grow dramatically, making up a good part of total economic output in some cases.[8] And in rich developing countries, the informal employment sector – consisting of unregistered workers, the black and grey markets and sometimes even slavery – has been difficult for state officials to eradicate.[9]

But I'm interested in something slightly different – namely, understanding why *unofficialdom* has suddenly become so central to the way mainstream jobs and commerce are organized.

I see it as a by-product of the economic liberalization that's inspired Western economic policy since the days of Thatcherism and Reaganomics up to the present. In a strange sort of way, the sex-for-rent scenario is a logical outcome of the free market doctrine so ardently embraced by Milton Friedman, Gary Becker and F. A. Hayek, although I'm guessing they wouldn't want to admit it. For them, central planning by government distorts the equilibrium of supply and demand. The role of figuring out how work, goods and services are distributed should be left to millions of private individuals to grapple with alone. Enterprise and the price mechanism (a.k.a. cash) are far more efficient for allocating resources compared to distant and lethargic state bureaucrats. Moreover, anybody ought to be free to offer any service they like if there is a consumer willing to pay for it. Licences, registration and certification are barriers to open competition and entrepreneurship. If a service turns out bad, we don't need a government shaking a stick. The customer will simply go elsewhere and the market will automatically correct itself.

In short, why do we need to waste taxpayers' dollars on local housing authorities and government planning agencies when Craigslist can far more effectively distribute those plentiful spare bedrooms in London, Chicago or Glasgow? All at the touch of a button . . . and perhaps a little more besides, as the listings above indicate.

Land of Strangers?

This brand of unregulated, almost secretive, individualism is a key ideological driver behind the widespread Uberization of society we've witnessed over the last few years. This is where workers, for example, are deemed independent business owners, a logic that has also been embraced by the so-called 'sharing economy' and what some have dubbed 'platform capitalism'.[10] However, there's a significant divergence between the academic models of free market capitalism (as envisaged by the neoclassical and mainstream economic tradition inaugurated by the Chicago School) and their messy, real-world implications. According to Hayek, for example, free market capitalism is great because it *anonymizes* and depersonalizes the actors involved.[11] Complete strangers can come together and trade goods and services and then depart. There's no complicated baggage or hang-ups involved. At the end of the day, business is business.

As we mentioned in the Introduction, Hayek considered this a good thing because money apparently blinds us to the particular 'whom' behind the transaction, solving a lot of problems in relation to favouritism and bias. Here, there are no personal whims or prejudice to contend with, which Hayek connected with government bureaucrats prone to cronyism and special interest groups (workers, the disabled and racial minorities are singled out, rather than corporate-sponsored think tanks, of course). Due to the emphasis placed on cash anonymity, critics of neoliberal capitalism have lamented the veritable social desert that subsequently evolves, an unwelcoming 'land of strangers' that recognizes only the colour of your money and very little else.[12]

But, as the rent-for-sex example illustrates, this cold cash nexus might certainly be transactional and calculating, but it's not anonymous. Sex (and god knows what else) is being exchanged, after all. While the 'live-in bi plaything' (to quote yet another Craigslist ad) appreciates it's all just an economic arrangement, she must still engage with a massive amount of personal and arbitrary judgement. To a lesser extent, the same blend of cash objectivity and arbitrary discrimination is experienced in many facets of the economy. The agency worker in a bar, for example, feels the need to ingratiate herself with the boss in order to get another shift. The Uber driver seeks a high rating from a passenger. Or take the corporate employee who feels compelled to spend hours in the company gym listening to a supervisor tell bad jokes because their promotion depends upon it.

Didn't the recent exposé of office life at Amazon's headquarters perfectly capture what we are dealing with here?[13] An electronic 360-degree feedback tool transformed the annual performance review into an almost daily event, with staff encouraged to comment secretly about their colleagues. Some alleged the system was manipulated by workers to crush each other emotionally in this dog-eat-dog environment. While the corporate culture officially emphasized quantifiable and impartial data, the metrics literally burrowed under employees' skin – one 'Amazonian' spoke of a stress-induced stomach ulcer: 'It's as if you've got the C.E.O. of the company in bed with you at 3 a.m. breathing down your neck.'[14] On one level, the management ethos is icy cold and impersonal. But on another, it's so 'hot' and personal that it keeps workers up at night dreading the next day.

From here, it is easy to see what *efficiency* really means in neoclassical economics, a concept that's been endlessly glorified in its lexicon. We are not really dealing with cost-effective input/out transactions, but a situation where someone else (preferably far away from the action) ends up bearing most or all the costs involved – typically employees, the unemployed, renters and other less-power players. This too transposes what ought to be simple impersonal forces (e.g., money) into a painfully intimate ordeal. One reason for this is that the average person now functions as a human *shock absorber* for an unsustainable paradigm. What kind of 'shocks' do I mean? Take the case of Cherie Nolan. She was employed by delivery firm Hermes for nine years and had a 'life from hell' as a result.[15] Cherie started her shift at 5.30 a.m. each day and kept working for as long she could. But soon the 'negative externalities' began to catch up with her, spilling over into her personal life. Senior management had little sympathy, of course:

I haven't had a holiday in seven years, and I only took three weekends off – when my grandad, great-uncle and granny died . . . When my granny's hearse was coming up the road, my field manager was still ringing me, telling me I needed to get back to work. When my son was born, I worked on the Monday, gave birth on the Tuesday night and on Wednesday I heard they were trying to get people to take over my rounds. I ended up going back to work on the Friday, three days after giving birth, because I was so frightened I'd lose my job.[16]

The comment vividly demonstrates how the crisis of work is also a crisis of the household, since the two domains cannot be separated, as recent writers have pointed out.[17] But we need to go further. For doesn't this case answer a perplexing question about Uber-jobs? Not why there are so many . . . *but so few.* If this is the cheapest method for organizing work, then shouldn't it be literally everywhere by now? No, because the social body as a whole simply couldn't take the hit, so it remains a fringe development, channelled to certain socio-economic groups and closely managed by the state to assist broader socio-political interests.

The biographical horrors described by Cherie Nolan are invisible in mainstream econometric models, impossible to capture in equations like $Q = f(X_1, X_2, X_3, ..., X_n)$. Deaths in the family and giving birth are strictly a private matter, stuff you keep to yourself. To fill the void that lies between the 'production function' equation (depicted above) and the fear-ridden life of Cherie Nolan, concepts like 'Pareto's optimality' and the 'social premium' are cited, where both Hermes and Cherie are declared winners. One can almost hear the cant as industry leaders gather at an expensive black-tie event: if Hermes didn't employ people like Cherie Nolan, then she'd be jobless and thus much worse off. The company is doing her a massive favour. They make a nice profit in the process, no doubt. But doesn't that help Cherie as much as it does the business? And so on.

To cut through this business bullshit, we need an equation of loss – a theorem to counteract the abstract idealism that has clouded the minds of so many economists and policy-makers today. It would permit us to theorize the Amazon and Hermes examples from the victim's point of view, and demonstrate how this strange brew of economic intimacy and cash callousness is suffocating the modern workforce. Whereas the doctrine of extreme individualism continues to be promoted as a vehicle of freedom, it's really just a neat formula for *privatizing* the symptoms of financial dispossession, hiding these dirty realities, ushering them out of the public limelight and beyond democratic scrutiny.

Too Close for Comfort

The trouble with the dominant neoclassical worldview is this. Its followers stubbornly assume that the anonymous logic of money functions in a vacuum. There are no concentrations of private power, no relations of dependency or exploited tenants. The seedy and humiliating reality that so many are forced to endure is radically discounted. It buys into the utopian fantasy popularized by the Chicago School, insisting that everyone is competing on a level playing field, imperceptible to each other as they act through the razor-thin medium of money. However, once we situate the economic actor – particularly the isolated and unprotected worker with nothing to sell but her labour time . . . and body – amidst concrete power relationships with insurmountable odds, then we are better positioned to understand why informality is moving centre-stage.

Figure 1 depicts the intersection I am exploring. Along one axis we have the level of formalization involved. The word 'formal' derives from the Latin word 'formalis' or 'forma', and trades on the tenet of universality as opposed to particular cases. A formal situation is governed by a *code* and confers a degree of officiousness, meaning the code must be applied consistently regardless of the specific issue at hand.[18] Expertise and credentials also become important here. They denote an element of professionalism (and legal legitimacy in public organizations).

Informal interactions, on the other hand, are more casual, unplanned and ad hoc. They're what might be called sub-regulated, since no social space is ever totally ruleless, for obvious reasons. Order

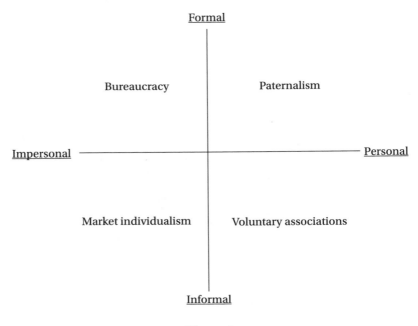

Figure 1

arises between people on a dyadic basis. Individual choice and private preferences expressed at the micro-level are key here.

The second axis gauges whether the relationship is personal or not. At one end, we have what Hayek calls the impersonal 'cash nexus', which is governed by private, individual commerce.[19] This social interaction is founded on generalizable exchange, meaning the personal is less salient than hard cash – hence, the fetishization of anonymity in neoclassical economic thought, especially in Hayek's work. Money allows a diverse range of activities to be measured against a single standard, no matter how idiosyncratic the people, goods and services involved may be. This is why neoclassical economists believe that sellers and purchasers in a well-functioning labour market are technically invisible to each other. Importantly, a significant shift occurs here, moving us from liberalism to neoliberalism. In the past, we assumed that public office and/or legality were the best tools for realizing the dictum *sine ira et studio* (without anger or fondness). Not anymore. Now it is the private money economy that takes a leading role in this regard.

At the more personal end of the spectrum are social relations that are uniquely specific and emotionally anchored in particular encounters between people. In contradistinction to the impersonal cash nexus – which condenses life into a monocratic and infinitely exchangeable calculus – personal interactions are noted for their singular and irreplaceable qualities. Localized social contact and preferences are salient.

We can now derive four organizational forms. Firstly, the classic bureaucracy is formal and impersonal, be it in the public or private sector. Secondly, paternalism gives a more personal, emotional touch to formal hierarchies. The US management fad of building clan-like corporate cultures and commitment programmes is a good example. While we're all meant to be friends and authentically ourselves, most workers understand that ultimately there is a boss who pays your wages and can fire you.[20] Non-capitalist organizations such as the Mondragon co-operative in Spain and others in Latin America fit this category too, albeit in a more democratic milieu.[21] The third type of organization weds personal interactions with informality, including voluntary associations, syndicalism, free societies and even cartels that trade in illicit goods. These organizations tend to be voluntary and rather private in orientation (e.g., secret societies, clubs, etc.).

It's the fourth category that I'm interested in. Market individualism is highly impersonal in that it's driven by cash exchange and yet, due to this private facet (and especially the uneven power relationships that define the economy, particularly between worker and employer), it

naturally gravitates towards informality too. This dynamic is accentu-
ated when the neoliberal state takes a back seat and certain regulatory
laws are weakened.

The Disappearing Object of Economics

The term 'market individualism' is perhaps misleading because neither markets nor individualism are peculiar to neoliberal capitalism,
or even capitalism *per se*. But, unlike other societies that had a time
and place for local market activities (a town square, for example), neoclassical economists, particularly Chicago School thinkers, sought to
use it as the guiding metaphor for society as a whole, crowding out
all other narratives. Can a society actually function as one gigantic
marketplace? James K. Galbraith makes an important point in this
regard. When neoliberal thinkers mention the 'market', they're not
really referring to a 'thing' but a *negation*:

> It is a word to be applied to the context of any transaction so long
> as that transaction is not directly dictated by the state. The word
> has no content of its own because it is defined simply, and for
> reasons of politics, by what it is not. The market is the nonstate,
> and thus it can do everything the state can do with none of the
> procedures or rules or limitations.[22]

We can see how the ideology operates. All that *isn't* the state is
automatically deemed ethically superior until proven otherwise. As for
governments, they only really excel at political favouritism and backroom plotting, making the system unfair and capricious.[23] However,
my argument is this. As the public sphere and democratic influence

recede, business is inevitably pushed underground both literally and symbolically. In the parlance of founding Chicago School economist Frank Knight (often repeated by Donald Trump), life is about private citizens making deals.[24] Indeed, if the state must exist at all, it has to be fundamentally 'self-denying' and geared towards regulatory 'disarmament', to use the terminology of libertarian Anthony de Jasay.[25]

As we have seen, the Chicago School's antidote to 'big government' was the impartiality of money. When combined with the price mechanism, the theory argued, cash exchange allows a spontaneous and undesigned social order (or 'catallaxy') to emerge from a multitude of diverse values and goals. Individual freedom is protected by the objectivity of an impersonal marketplace, which is largely disinterested in the personal qualities and circumstances of those involved. However, don't we see something rather different unfold in practice? Just look at the various parts of the formula. Private arrangements are now inscrutable to the law and regulatory protections. Solitary individuals are essentially on their own as they enter into negotiations with other private parties, many of which are more powerful (a corporation, employer, landlord, etc.). And if we add to this the economic insecurity that's become a hallmark of austerity, including one-sided relationships of dependency, then a 'cult of informality' can soon take over. Deliveroo can always replace a rider – whereas the rider needs a job and their ability to walk away is minimal. As a result, riders are more likely to put up with treatment that other workers would baulk at. It's not difficult to see how this Uber-mentality of economic individualism can breed claustrophobic levels of familiarity in the workplace, housing market and more besides.

According to some observers, the purist version of neoliberalism probably died along with Friedman in 2006.[26] For even a cursory glance at economies in North America, Europe and Australasia – where leaders have been smitten by Chicago School economists over the last thirty-five years – reveals how far they've drifted away from free market ideals. The evidence speaks for itself. Supply-side policies have led to devastating market failures, requiring extensive state intervention to prop up private industry (e.g., banks, out-sourcing subcontractors, etc.), using dubious instruments like quantitative easing, company tax breaks and the transfer of outlandish levels of public funds to big business. Corporate monopolies and oligopolies have captured entire markets. Inherited wealth rather than merit determines your life chances, and the Randian myth of the 'self-made man' is now but a bad joke. Globalization is in ruins. Xenophobia is resurgent.

It's out of this dismal environment – characterized by a certain form of social wreckage – that the deformalization movement is born, the bastard child of neoliberalism, which is now changing the landscape of modern life.

Homo Contractus

The notion of 'unregulated capitalism' is also misleading, given that all forms of economic activity are regulated in some manner. And, furthermore, one may challenge my thesis concerning deformalization by asking why there continue to be so many contracts, laws (e.g., regarding patent infringements, intellectual property, etc.) and rules controlling almost everything we do today. It's a good question. However, the answer doesn't contradict my argument, but paints an even gloomier picture. There's no doubt that the leading personification of neoclassical economics – the mythic *Homo economicus*, or economic man – is now gravely sick and on life support. First, he transitioned into indebted man and that nearly finished him off.[27] But now another metamorphosis has taken place, transmuting him into contracted man, or *Homo contractus* . . . truly a lost cause.

A contract is a legally binding document. Neoclassical economists and jurists love them because they lock people in and allow agreements made at a specific time (a student loan given to an eighteen-year-old, for example) to track the individual far into the future. There's no escape. When someone signs a contract in the isolating environment of crisis capitalism (increasingly bereft of civic accountability), the root etymology of the word 'contract' – *contrahere* – comes to fruition in a terrifying manner. *Con* means 'with' or 'together', and *trahere*, 'to draw' or 'pull'.

Once again, none of this occurs in a vacuum. Economic inequality and desperation, for example, structure any legal agreement with a certain obligatory excess, an unspoken appreciation that other services will be on offer. If the formal part of the contract holds people to their promise, then the document's informal flipside implies that they're unconditionally *available* (a term, incidentally, that victims of Harvey Weinstein use). The root words 'pull', 'with' and 'to draw' take on extra meaning when filtered through Sugar Daddy Capitalism. If someone signs a zero-hours contract in a busy city restaurant, for example, there's nothing officially obliging her to flirt with the boss. But we all know what happens if she doesn't.[28] So she goes along with it. Or what about the psychological contract entered into by the rent-for-sex tenant? It is no coincidence that many Craigslist postings ask the applicant to read between the lines: 'this is a 1 bedroom flat that you will be sharing with me, the only bed is mine . . . you do the arithmetic!'

In other words, contractualization (in an economically exploitative context, at least) involves much more than simple legal objectivity. Documentation has a subjective life too, which requires us to read between the lines and practise expedience. That's probably why Uber, for example, don't even bother with formal contracts (since that would suggest drivers are indeed employees and thus subject to statutory laws) but settle with 'agreements' instead. They can change at any moment, although seldom in favour of workers. Such agreements operate as *ghost contracts*, which are even more controlling since workers get the worst of both worlds – the coercive features of a *de facto* contract, given how Uber-agreements are legally binding (e.g., its arbitration clauses banning class lawsuits), *and* the unsettling discretion of a loose agreement (with vice versa costs/benefits for employers). This is how an onerous form of informality can implicitly run alongside and support a highly impersonal social order that otherwise looks businesslike.[29]

Where does the state and its legal system stand in all of this, given its responsibility to enforce contracts? Contemporary statecraft has been deeply influenced by neoconservative law-makers, who are fervently anti-government, and staunch advocates of private individualism. With respect to employment law, for example, conservative legal scholar Richard Epstein calls this the long-awaited 'unlocking' of the workplace.[30] For him, unions, minimum wage laws and anti-discrimination policies are needless chains. Individuals ought to be able to negotiate their own terms and conditions in private. Now we all know where that leads. But this cultish attachment to the informal doesn't just affect workers in the gig economy. The trend is recoding many other occupations in significant ways – some of which were once considered the bastion of formality, including policing, teaching and so forth. In outlining how employment contract law has been 'liberalized' since the 1980s, it is the *public* shrinkage of the state-formation that Epstein singles out as decisive:

> the path to prosperity is not to create mandatory terms, not to create good faith bargaining obligations, and not to create a monopoly situation of any sort. Instead, it is to simply stand

aside, to let the contracts form as people will negotiate them, and then to enforce them in accordance with the terms by which they were written. Reform in this context constitutes a reduction in the level of legal interference with private arrangements.[31]

This view now generally underlines the majority of employment contracts in the Western world today. One must admire the incredible optimism with which Richard Epstein confers such moral probity upon these so-called 'private arrangements'. There are no rent-for-sex scenarios in his sanguine rendition of making ends meet in the new economy.

As the state reconfigures itself into a more punitive (rather than public) institution, upholding the interests of the rich and bullying everyone else, a vicious circle of deformalization develops, spiralling all the way down to the bottom of the class hierarchy: the struggling working poor and middle classes rightfully attempt to evade the harshest excesses of an uncaring government, mostly by escaping into the shadows of private economic life. This in turn sends a signal that *Homo contractus* really can look after him or herself, and sizeable parts of the public sphere are eroded further. Food safety regulations? Gone. Employee protection law? Gone. Publicly available mental health support? Gone.

Capitalism for Losers

It is not surprising that this partial collapse of organized formalism occurs just as economic inequality is reaching eye-watering levels. Today, the world's richest 1 per cent get 82 per cent of the wealth.[32] According to a 2017 'UBS/PwC Billionaires Report' – an analysis of wealth patterns prepared for the banking industry – in global terms, 'the total wealth of billionaires rose by 17% in 2016, up from USD5.1 trillion to USD6.0 trillion. There was a 10% rise in the number of billionaires globally to 1,542.'[33] One of the report's authors admitted that society hadn't seen wealth concentration like this since the Gilded Age in the early 1900s.[34] This visibly hastens a process of deformalization among the elite, because they can decouple from the nation-state and avoid public protocols (e.g., taxes, etc.). It isn't surprising that the report found 'billionaires are leveraging their networks' more than ever.[35] A lobby group specializing in tax avoidance even used language reminiscent of Harvey Weinstein's exploits when bragging about its 'superb penetration' at the highest levels of the British government.[36]

Wasn't this 'penetration' exemplified by PayPal co-founder Peter Thiel's activities in New Zealand?[37] He – like many other billionaires – see the small South Pacific country as a safe haven from the coming socio-economic apocalypse.[38] It's remote, sparsely populated and has few sites of military interest – the perfect location for a panic-room retreat in case the global system goes into meltdown. Thiel faced one major obstacle, however: New Zealand's strict laws on foreigners buying property. So, when Thiel successfully bought a 477-acre sheep station in the South Island, a journalist investigated the case. It turned out he was granted New Zealand citizenship in 2011, despite having spent only twelve days in the country. Thiel wasn't even in New Zealand when he became a Kiwi, attending a ceremony in Santa Monica instead. He'd promised the government that he would invest in the country's tech sector, and that was enough. It was later discovered that the billionaire had courted a number of New Zealand officials, including then Prime Minster (and ex-investment banker) John Key. Because Thiel wasn't actually planning to live in the country – a problem for the paperwork – he had citizenship conferred on him under the 'exceptional circumstances' rules.[39]

The Thiel case caused a scandal in New Zealand, for obvious reasons. Anyone else trying to apply for citizenship faces a major uphill battle, not to mention mountains of paperwork and a long wait. However, as Branko Milanović points out in his fascinating study of global inequality, the Uber-rich in Western economies have mostly detached themselves from the rest of society.[40] This is where sub-formal 'networks' and 'connections' come into play, which are typically plentiful for billionaires. Milanović demonstrates how bad inequality has got in relation to the employment sector. The skills and abilities possessed by the top 10 per cent of income-earners will soon *coincide* with those held by the middle classes. This is due to rising education levels as a whole. At the same time, however, social mobility (in terms of income) hasn't been so stagnant in years. The best jobs and highest salaries still go to the wealthy 10 per cent. That's because factors other than a university degree are now more important: 'chance and family background will play much more of a role than before . . . family endowments in wealth and, perhaps most importantly, connections, will matter more. One sees the effect of family money and networks in the United States very clearly in occupations where lots of power and money accrue.'[41]

Chicago School-inspired arguments for capitalism are notoriously tolerant of economic inequality.[42] Nobody is born the same. Some are simply better than others, and thus richer as a result. An egalitarian society would be ethically wrong for this reason, and so on. What continues to amaze me is this. Despite the growing scandals around income/wealth inequality that are threatening to rip our civilization apart, this neoliberal defence of inequality has *intensified* and not abated.[43] The rhetoric detracts from the fact that power rigs the system in favour of the rich from Day 1. By the same token, what worries me is not the prospect of people swallowing all this propaganda about how inequality is natural or good for us. No, what's dangerous is the way these otherwise eccentric claims can influence the *tone* (once again) of the broader discussion, like a tiny dust mote in the eye. For sure, even the most damaging conjectures of the far right aren't meant to enlist mass agreement – only to gently shift the parameters of debate and nudge our culture towards accepting (or at least expecting) what really ought to be unacceptable degrees of wealth-hoarding.

This sea change has had a caustic effect on public trust, because people feel unjustly disadvantaged if they *follow* the rules of the game. If no one else is, then why should I? This anti-civic attitude has always been there to some extent, but what's different now is how it cuts to the dark centre of our collective imagination. Gaming the system is the new normal, and you're a fool if you don't try – hence, the sad twilight of public democracy and the rise of Uber-sequestered individualism, where one's environment is perceived as terribly impersonal and yet hinged on knowing the right people.

The consequences are fairly obvious. Quickly fading today is the once-strident belief that skill, merit and education counted for something apropos future prospects and upward mobility.[44] Personal connections and patrimonial favours are more valuable than your objective abilities. For the very wealthy, this has always been the story. The middle classes, on the other hand, now realize that talent and ability are not enough. They relentlessly try to enrol themselves (and children) into the best social circles to get ahead. As for the poor – a struggling student or restaurant server – they're tempted to join a Sugar Daddy dating site to help pay tuition fees, and dream of being the next 'Pretty Woman' who's swept away by a wealthy stranger.[45] And if they need a place to live in the meantime, Craigslist has a wide range of opportunities, including this one:

£1 Cold Outside. Offering Free Flat (Bassetlaw)

Hi there,

Due to it being cold outside, I'm willing to offer a place in my small 1 bedroom flat for the right girl aged 16+ for mutual agreements. (Single mums welcome.)

Do you need a hot meal? A hot bath? Somewhere to wash your clothes? A brand new start in life? Well, it can be yours. You will be sharing my small 1 bedroom flat with me.

You would need to supply your own food. If you require me to supply you some food, this will be a totally different arrangement.

Please tell me a little bit about you and please send a picture of you.

Chapter Two

Sugar Daddy Capitalism

Brandon Wade (born 1970 in Singapore as Lead Wey) said he came up with his new business idea when down on his luck in the romance department. He'd been cruising dating sites with little success.[1] Wade's awkward and IT-nerd demeanour didn't help. Then his mother imparted some advice that came as a revelation: 'one day when you're successful and generous, the girls will come'. His main handicap was confidence and opportunity. After graduating with a Master's degree from MIT in electrical engineering, Wade had a great job with a six-figure salary, but no way to hook up with the beautiful girls he longed to date. So he started his own online 'Sugar Daddy' dating sites, WhatsYourPrice.com and SeekingArrangement.com.

The business model is simple. Wealthy older men (whom Wade termed 'Sugar Daddies') frequently want to date younger women (or 'Sugar Babies') but have no way to facilitate the arrangement. And young women are attracted to males who might help cover their college tuition and living expenses, wine and dine them in expensive restaurants and buy gifts. After the two parties meet online, they agree to a fee for an encounter. The unspoken motivator for Sugar Daddies is that some kind of sexual experience will occur, whereas Sugar Babies are in it for the money.[2]

The idea was a hit. Today Wade presides over a multimillion-dollar business with 3.2 million users in the USA alone, and an expanding customer base.[3] He's added similar websites to his portfolio, including SeekingMillionaire.com and MissTravel.com (which, according to the official website, helps pair 'generous travellers who hate to travel alone with attractive travellers who would love the opportunity to travel the world for free').

Wade says that the typical Sugar Daddy has an annual income of US$200,000 and spends about $3,000 a month on a Sugar Baby.[4] Around 40 per cent of the men are married, whereas 44 per cent of Sugar Babies are college students.[5] When asked about the philosophy behind the business, Wade became infamous for his rather instrumental take on romance. At the end of the day, he suggests, WhatsYourPrice.com is about economics . . . supply and demand:

> love is a concept invented by poor people. Love at first sight that sends shivers down your spine is a fairy-tale, and it doesn't last forever.[6]

By remodelling love into a simple transactional affair, according to Wade, partners avoid the possessiveness, drama and irrational clashes that so often mar conventional relationships:

> Traditional relationships are based on possessiveness and self-ishness. As I look at the future of traditional relationships, I see divorces, heartbreaks and broken families. Marriage is messy, but divorce is even messier. Yet marriage is not the only path to happiness or financial security. An arrangement can provide the same benefits as a marriage without the risk . . . By encouraging people to find and negotiate an arrangement, we hope to create modern relationships based on open-mindedness, open communication, brutal honesty and transparent expectations.[7]

It wasn't just these views about marriage and romance that generated controversy around Brandon Wade. For some, his business model bore a close resemblance to another well-known profession: *prostitution*.[8] Wade was labelled an 'e-pimp' for promoting what appeared to be sex work.[9] His dating sites were nothing but a front for the exchange of sexual services, cloaked in the language of 'dating' to make it look more palatable for Sugar Daddies and Sugar Babies.

Dinner Date with Caligula

Sugar Babies have been interviewed to see if they feel like sex workers. Is the dating genuine or are they escorts in disguise? Take Serena Cervantes.[10] She was once employed as a maid but the income couldn't cover the costs of her university education. Things got so bad at one point that Serena spent time in a homeless shelter. Then she joined SugarDaddies.com and was finally able to make ends meet: 'In my heart of hearts I don't really like the situation. Right now it's a survival mechanism.'[11]

But is sex always involved? According to another report: yes, usually. Sarah and Marilyn became Sugar Babes while studying in London.[12] Both were desperate for cash. Sarah mentions her first date: 'I felt like a whore the entire time. I knew everyone was looking at me like I was a whore.' Marilyn said, 'every guy I went on a date with eventually asked me to fuck'.[13] While they didn't feel obliged to have sex with their date, Marilyn concludes on a dark note: 'you just feel so used after a while and impure. There is a sense of purity that's lost when you commodify yourself. If you sleep with too many people, too – at least for me.'[14] For another Sugar Baby called Coco, using the website was camouflage for sex work. When asked if it was mandatory to have sex with her date, she said, 'Yeah. For me, it's just like a normal relationship, the only difference is I get money . . . [but] don't get me wrong, it's selling yourself'.[15]

The confusion about whether Sugar Babies are sex workers or not exemplifies the trend I'm seeking to understand in this book: the deformalization movement at the centre of Western capitalism. As we have already noted, rules and regulations still abound, of course. But certain shifts are occurring in how commerce is organized, which Brandon Wade's business model epitomizes. To see how this functions, let's take a typical Sugar Daddy encounter. The Sugar Baby offers to sell a date online. An auction ensues. A fee is negotiated. The two parties meet and (awkward) sex is usually the upshot. So it ought to count as prostitution . . . only it exists *without* the legal status and protections that registered sex workers otherwise receive in many Western countries. All those hard-won rights are sidestepped in an instant. And since the boundary between working and living is blurred beyond recognition, the job itself (if it is to be labelled that) disappears into the recesses of private life, far beyond the prying eyes of government agencies.

Share . . . or Else!

Brandon Wade's dating sites might be an extreme version of the deformalization process – something of an outlier. But don't we see something similar happening – albeit to a lesser extent – in the so-called gig or 'collaborative economy' more generally? The Airbnb host isn't a registered hotelier, but someone like you and me with a spare room. As opposed to traditional taxi-drivers who are trained and certified, the Uber-worker is just an ordinary person with a car willing to drive you across town for a fee.

The ongoing transformation of labour into ghost-like Uberized roles has been significant in many countries around the world. Even regular jobs now include expectations inspired from the platform economy: to be always on-call, constantly worry about what's happening at the office and skip the kid's school play . . . all of this sunders the conventional 9-to-5 we used to know. Because seeking an income bleeds into everyday living in such a thorough manner, there are as yet no sociological classifications or legal categories to pin down exactly what's going on. Business school academic Arun Sundararajan suggests that the rise of 'crowd-based capitalism' and peer-to-peer commerce could even hasten the end of employment.[16] The on-demand economy has been particularly effective in dismantling the once-impervious compartmentalization of work, where it was separated from other activities (education, family, etc.). Now people *are* their jobs, whether formally checked in or not. Securing an income is a way of life that is both disciplinary (you are punished if you miss a shift) and unrelenting (it never stops), no matter how much it disguises itself in the charitable, Bono-like semantics of the sharing economy.

The origins of this intense economization of every aspect of existence, including the rise of boundless labour, can be traced back to ideas posited in neoclassical economics. In his 1944 capitalist manifesto – *The Road to Serfdom* – F. A. Hayek foresees business models of the future, especially ones like SeekingArrangement.com and MissTravel.com.[17] The book argues that central planning by the state and its army of bureaucrats inevitably ends up violating our personal and civic freedoms. Sure, minimal laws are needed to uphold the 'rules of the game' and enforce contracts. But governments are often tempted to go much further and manage people as homogeneous masses, thus frustrating the unique goals that some may choose to pursue as lone individuals. For Hayek, no central authority could ever authentically know or accommodate the vast number of preferences held by millions of private citizens. The values of modern man are too diverse and disparate. So it's better to allow each person to choose their own path freely.

For this reason, Hayek considers generalizable terms like 'social welfare' and 'common good' disingenuous. There are no common interests that 100 per cent of society share. These terms are more reflective of special interest groups (e.g. trade unions) that have lobbied the government to impose their objectives on everyone else. When we hear politicians use universal concepts such as the 'social good' to justify laws and regulations, they're in fact partisan policies that benefit only certain people. For this reason, Hayek continues, a degree of arbitrariness enters the statecraft process: for example, setting national income levels; constraining employer recruitment choices via anti-discrimination laws; regulating business activities; insisting that unions have representation on corporate boards. All of this deters our entrepreneurial verve because the situation is predetermined by distant officials. There is no room for risky and independent enterprise. No one can get ahead if we're all the same.

Let's follow Hayek onto even thinner ice.

As opposed to having a central planner meddling in our business, he recommends the state provide nothing more than a wafer-thin, skeletal legal code – but with a difference. Unlike conventional jurisprudence in this area, Hayek talks about a 'Meta-Legal-Principle'. What on earth does that mean? Well, not only are their fewer laws, but law-makers must actively delimit their own powers, not enable them though endless rule-making.[18] In a society populated by self-regulating individuals minding their own business, legislators should encourage their own redundancy. The baseline of all freedom is each person's ability to do whatever they decide (within minimum legal parameters), a philosophy of capitalist libertarianism that Hayek advocated as a matter of urgency: 'it is this recognition of the individual as the ultimate judge of his ends, the belief that as far as possible his own views ought to govern his actions, that forms the essence of the individualist position'.[19] Hayek uses the analogy of a roadmap to explain his point. The state might ensure that the cartography is accurate. But it would be wrong to tell you *where* on the map to drive since that's entirely your choice. This is where money enters the picture for Hayek. Personal liberty can only really be ensured via the *unknowable* transactions of the price mechanism – even if expressed in rather personal ways, as we see with Brandon Wade's dating websites and his attempt to overcome shyness with beautiful women. He'd rather have the size of his income do the talking than his physical appearance or background. And the internet makes that much easier for obvious reasons.

Similarly, Hayek advocated what he saw as the impersonal, spontaneous and anonymous forces of the marketplace as the natural medium of money, as opposed to some busybody state functionary sticking their nose in our lives. Objective cash price is the only issue of importance in the society envisaged by Hayek and the Chicago School, since it liberates people from the subjective judgements of others (e.g., tradition, prejudice, religious mores, public policy, etc.) and allows them to realize their unique preferences in an unhindered fashion.

Natural Born Capitalists

Hayek's rather cold argument allows him to draw some bold conclusions, whose sad echo we see in the Uber-brutalism of late capitalism today.

Firstly, he chastises critics who believe that the economy should be contained or separated from the rest of society, perhaps in the name of pursuing more edifying goals such as the arts (regardless of their commercial viability) or exempting the poor from market forces (e.g., via welfare). For Hayek, the economy is not a detachable sphere that can be placed in a secondary position ... it encompasses *all of life*. Economics is everything and it would be naïve to think otherwise. One reason Hayek takes this stance is because he believed cash commerce – preferably practised in a decentralized environment – is the only way individual freedom can be truly secured. And because we *always* want to be free – as expressed in our choices and preferences – the economy must always be with us too, no matter how 'undignified' that might sound. In this argument, we see the seeds for subsequent ideas in the Chicago School – such as human capital theory, which notoriously boiled down all individual activities, even drug addiction, to their economic utility. What does getting an education, choosing a partner or following a particular career path mean in terms of financial returns? Life is only about money, which isn't merely a normative injunction (it enhances personal freedom) but an ontological axiom (it's how reality works). Perhaps ironically then, in light of Brandon Wade, this is truly economics without the romance.

Hayek links this premise to the idol of personal responsibility. Once central planners begin to take care of our economic circumstances (e.g., protecting us from unemployment or providing pensions), we unwittingly hand over a significant degree of control. Many people wrongly 'believe that anything which, like economic planning, affects only our economic interests, cannot seriously interfere with the more basic values of life'.[20] This belief is a big mistake, according to Hayek. That's why insecurity and the possibility of losing everything is the price we must pay for personal freedom, an idea we see millions of freelancers in the USA and UK embodying to this day. Hayek views insecurity as a badge of honour.

As for the second implication, which is a corollary of the first: the open marketplace that safeguards our anonymous and personal freedoms should not be delimited in any way. Presaging Wade's most popular website – WhatsYourPrice.com – Hayek argues: 'in a competitive society almost anything can be had at a price . . . that life and health, beauty and virtue, honour and peace of mind, can often be preserved only at considerable material cost is as undeniable as that we all are sometimes not prepared to make the material sacrifices necessary to protect those high values'.[21] Putting aside topics such as slavery, Hayek claims that questions of 'higher values' cannot be excused from the cash nexus because that would be the first step towards inviting a higher authority to decide what's best for us. And the endgame is totalitarianism.

Hayek's strained logic played out in latter variants of neoliberal reason. In microeconomics, for example, Chicago School scholar Gary Becker famously claimed that even our most intimate pastimes – love and marriage – are best understood through the lens of utility maximization and rational choice theory.[22] The temptation to view marriage as a non-economic, romantic endeavour is illogical, given the vast sums involved over a lifetime. And the same message has slowly seeped into how people behave today. For example, 'assortative mating' (where high-income individuals marry partners from their same socioeconomic bracket) has dramatically increased in the USA and UK since the 1980s.[23] This has in turn had a major impact on income and wealth inequality, since people seldom 'marry down', but stick to their own kind.

It is only in the context engendered by these ideas that MissTravel.com and similar business systems could gain traction. The Hayekian mission of commercializing life *in toto* (including what economists once termed 'nonmonetary variables') especially resonates with Sugar Daddy capitalism. Why should a Sugar Daddy waste scarce resources searching for a partner the old-fashioned way when there's an app that can *directly* match him with the girl he desires with no strings attached? Moreover – and following Gary Becker's human capital theory – we can now see why some industry leaders argue that WhatsYourPrice.com isn't far removed from what happens in normal relationships anyway. Whether we like it or not, the 'cash nexus' is integral to dating and romance. What is different, according to Brandon Wade, is the honesty with which his websites view this monetary dimension, putting it on the same footing as other business transactions. Sugardaddie.com CEO Steven Pasternack makes a similar point:

I helped my wife get through school, I pay for the bills, take her on trips, buy her nice gifts. I guess you could say a lot of married guys are Sugar Daddies without them realizing it. I think you can say basically any guy who wants to impress a woman is a Sugar Daddy.[24]

That might be a dark thought. But the underlying reality is darker still. Sugar Daddy capitalism ultimately conveys a theory of human nature that keys into Hayek's view of people as money-chasing animals. It is telling (and apt) that US business school professors frequently open their lectures with a famous George Bernard Shaw story to set the tone. The playwright once asked a prominent actress whether she would sleep with him for a million dollars. 'Yes', she smiled. He then followed up with another question: 'What about five dollars?' 'Certainly not sir, what do you think I am?', she replied, clearly insulted by the proposition. Shaw swiftly replied: 'We've already established that – now we're just haggling over price.' At the end of the day, according to neoclassical economics, we're all whores at heart and will compromise our most cherished values without a thought . . . if the price is right.[25]

Platform Perverts

At the forefront of the Hayekian approach is the notion that we should embrace the faceless mechanism of money and the impersonal forces of the marketplace. Hayek articulated the idea most clearly in relation to law and the state. Only a basic rule of law is required in this utopia of capitalist individualism. The state should protect the sanctity of private property, enforce contracts, punish fraudulent behaviour and so forth. But it exists mainly to provide legal certainty so that everyone can make their own plans via the anonymous signals of the market. Under this system, people remain unknown to the state and its agencies. Government functions like a croupier in a casino, never able to foretell who'll win next. Hayek unpacks the argument in more detail:

> formal rules are thus merely instrumental in the sense that they are expected to be useful to yet unknown people, for purposes for which these people will decide to use them, and in circumstances which cannot be foreseen in detail . . . they do not involve a choice between particular ends or particular people, because we cannot know beforehand by who and in what way they will be used.[26]

Hayek's weak or 'ecological' legal formalism is not meant to play favourites. For example, any attempt to legislate for equality apropos ethnic minorities or to guarantee a minimum wage for workers is strictly prohibited under this brand of formalism. Hayek goes to great lengths to defend the stance. The way he sees it, any form of discrimination (good or bad) introduces an element of arbitrariness into the task of government. Sure, it may favour particular interest groups today. But it could all easily go the other way tomorrow, depending on the whims of the central planner.

But here an important slippage occurs. Hayek's weak formalism seeks to complement the anonymity achieved by pure monetary exchange. Each individual transaction is a unique and private matter. Note in the quote above, for example, that Hayek doesn't want to know what your personal interests are, nor the specific arrangements you've made with an employer or landlord, as long as they're consonant with the rule of law. Legalism functions as an unobtrusive dome under which almost anything can happen in a free market. But let's take closer a look at what this anonymity entails. To whom exactly do I become anonymous and unidentifiable as I go about my business? Does the ageing Sugar Daddy remain anonymous to his eighteen-year-old Sugar Baby? No, of course not. They're having sex after all.

Clearly it is the *government* that Hayek has in mind. The nominal legal formalism posited in *The Road to Serfdom* and *The Constitution of Liberty* is actually just a neat way to permit everyday economic activity to remain inscrutable to the gaze of the state. Just as the price mechanism is said to solve the enigma of limited knowledge that dogs central planning, Hayek's theory of law sought to solve the problem of personal freedom through the concept of anonymity, a space where Sugar Babies and Sugar Daddies are left alone to get on with their business, unburdened by taxes or statutory requirements – hence my central argument. Although he didn't intend to, Hayek's economic philosophy tacitly encourages the personalization of economic relations, so that it weirdly commingles with the nameless flows of money. His proposed cash formalism – 'without regard for persons' – was in practice a rationale for securing the opposite – namely, ad hoc private interactions that lie beyond the purview of the state since they're none of its business.

Every now and then, we can see signs of this informalism creeping into Hayek's narrative, waving its arms in the wings but never coming out into the open. This is especially evident regarding his opinions about the employment relationship. Of course, he vehemently opposes state intervention with respect to minimum wage laws or welfare for the unemployed. Such policies create a moral hazard (or perverse disincentives) because why would people work any harder if they are guaranteed a certain wage? Or why work at all if the state will support you? When it comes to jobs and occupations, the government, unions and professional associations should all step aside and allow two private individuals – the employer and employee – to sort out their own arrangement.

This is certainly an extreme view, but it has left its mark on how modern work is now approached in many OECD countries. Some sixty years later, Hayek's meditations about what a proper employment relationship entails are suspiciously congruent with today's gig economy and zero-hours contracts. For example, in the quote below, he's criticizing the government policy of setting industry pay levels and using aptitude tests to help select candidates for specific jobs (a once-popular Keynesian governance policy). For Hayek, such measures kill individual incentive and undermine flexibility:

when the authority fixes the remuneration for a whole category and the selection among the candidates is made by an objective test, the strength of [the candidate's] desire for the job will count for very little. The person whose qualifications are not of the standard type, or whose temperament is not of the ordinary kind, will no longer be able to come to special arrangements with an employer whose dispositions will fit in with his special needs: the person who prefers irregular hours or even a happy-go-lucky existence with a small and perhaps uncertain income to a regular routine will no longer have a choice.[27]

Doesn't the rationale perfectly fit the mania of Uberization we see spreading today, not to mention the ethos behind WhatsYourPrice. com? State regulators must stand back and ensure that bargaining occurs on a local, one-to-one basis. The reason why, according to neoclassical economics, is because each situation is different and incommensurable, even in the same industry. Indeed, *even in the same organization*, given how different each person is. As a result, the idiosyncratic details of workers' individual circumstances remain unknowable to external authorities. This might look clean and unimposing in theory. But the reality is somewhat different, especially if Harvey Weinstein decides to make a surprise visit. At any rate, work becomes both intimate and transactional – deeply personal and yet numbingly instrumental. Hayek believed he'd found a method for expunging discretion and arbitrariness from economic behaviour, but ends up welcoming it in through the backdoor . . . and a much worse form of it, to boot.

An elementary flaw in Hayekian economics is its terrible approach to power. Because the state is deemed a collective entity, it's instantly assumed to be on an endless power trip. Domination is everywhere – whereas the private sphere (under market capitalism) is made up of free individuals who negotiate outside of hierarchies. The anonymity of money dilutes and disperses undue influence. Domination simply vanishes. Of course, private corporations and wealthy individuals never operate in this Hayekian fashion. This is a dreamtime version of capitalism. Being on the coalface of neoliberal realism isn't a walk through the tulips as Hayek and the Chicago School imagined. We only need to return to WhatsYourPrice.com to note the dynamic that unfolds in these *secretized* and covert work situations. One Sugar Baby admits in an interview that 'it's very dangerous, it means they think you're their slave, you're their pet, so they can do whatever they want'.[28]

Similar complaints of egregious authority (above and beyond what's financially necessary) is common among 'gig economy' workers. In a climate that encourages chronic dependence and uncertainty, it's easy to see how 'getting on' with your supervisor – and we all know what that means – takes a central role. For example, here is a woman describing what it's like working in a London bar that uses insecure contracts: 'A bar manager took to calling one of the girls "Treacle". The 19-year-old student was told she had "great wrist action" as she mixed a G&T. She visibly squirmed when he asked her to "stop flirting with him", but she felt powerless.'[29] Sexual harassment and patrimony are not new, of course. But something else is occurring here that is fairly novel. This (all too) personal familiarity in the work environment is underscored by an impersonal cash transaction. Money itself invariably takes on sleazy qualities as a result – not only impersonal but *yucky*. What the Chicago School thought were antithetical logics in their theoretical frameworks actually merge into a singular force in reality.

Survival of the Filthiest

Hayek foresees a number of objections to his position. By addressing each in turn, he then tries to entrench his dubious approach even further, sometimes testing the limits of credibility.

For example, imagine that I desire a particular job – such as piloting a commercial airliner – but don't have the requisite qualifications. Or perhaps I encounter race and gender discrimination that reduces my chances of promotion. Should the government step in to help me get ahead . . . perhaps offering a training scholarship or equal opportunities programme? No. Unfettered market competition should be the only arbiter because money ultimately creates the most efficient outcome. I might borrow the money in order to access pilot training, which will enhance my future earnings measurably. Discriminatory employers will go out of business because they limit the talent pool from which to recruit the best workers. The market has a corrective function in this respect:

> a weakly boy who has set his heart on a job where his weakness handicaps him, as well as in general the apparently less able or less suitable, are not necessarily excluded in a competitive society; if they value the position sufficiently, they will frequently be able to get a start by a financial sacrifice and will later make good through qualities which at first are not so obvious.[30]

The problem here is Hayek's wilful blindness to the degenerative influence of class inequality and its erosion of meritocracy, which is evident now more than ever. People from an already wealthy background usually end up with the best-paying jobs. But a further pernicious implication can be seen in Hayek's argument. What does he mean by 'financial sacrifice'? No doubt today we would recognize this as the burden of student debt. It has practically crippled a generation of middle-class people who desired a better life (by obtaining a degree) but couldn't afford the tuition fees.[31] And from here, of course, it's just a small step before we arrive back at WhatsYourPrice.com and the world of Sugar Daddy economics.

It's easy to understand why the rich continue to adore Hayek. What more could a major firm want than to negotiate with isolated and insecure workers on an individual basis rather than as a group? Or a large property management company in London which is free to treat its desperate tenants however it chooses since the state wants no part in regulating the private rental market? When put into practice,

Hayek's libertarian philosophy basically *presents* and then *exposes* the individual economic agent (the worker, the student, a tenant) to the crucible of cash judgement. Indeed, this socio-political production of unsheltered individualism is the centrepiece of neoliberal governance. And in the realm of employment, people aren't even sheltered by a place of employment (in the case of Uberized jobs and Sugar Babies), let alone unions or state legislation.

The global corporate elite pounced on Hayek's elevation of anonymity for other reasons. It's no coincidence that a defining characteristic of global finance capitalism is the tremendous level of economic activity occurring beyond the state-formation. The sums involved are incredible. Take shadow banking, for example. A 2015 investigation by the Financial Stability Board found that unregulated transactions had risen to $80 trillion (£53 trillion), equivalent to 60 per cent of the GDP of the twenty-six participating jurisdictions.[32] Tax avoidance follows the same pattern, as revealed in the 2017 Paradise Papers leak.[33] And then there's the criminal element that is inevitably drawn to these invisible zones that Hayek helped legitimate. Money laundering and trade misinvoicing have reached epic proportions.[34] For us 99 per-centers, Hayek's rendition of anonymity is about making it easier for 'Treacle's' amorous supervisor to flirt (a.k.a. harass) with her unimpeded. Whereas for plutocrats and their shady shell companies, it's an escape route from tax liabilities.

A new economic horizon emerges in global commerce at this point – one that might be labelled dark capitalism, a parallel mode of trade that is outside the normal jurisdiction of the national (and international) legal apparatus. Its modus operandi is simple and can be discerned by the following thought-experiment. What are we finally left with if we strip down the idea of an anything-goes free market to its essential components, as recommended by Hayek? No state. The supply and demand of goods and services totally unregulated. Few norms of best practice or standards that might dissuade people from following their heart's desire. A world governed purely by the price system, inhabited by strangers cloaked in anonymity as they forge private arrangements.

Jamie Bartlett helps us answer this question in his book *The Dark Net*, a fascinating investigation of the secret internet server.[35] Due to sophisticated encryption techniques (and a Tor browser), it is impossible to identify users on this network. Ironically enough, the US government developed the dark web with this anonymity in mind. It released the software to the public, thinking that pro-democracy activists would use it to undermine autocratic governments in China, Iran and elsewhere. Instead, it's now the medium of choice for traders in illegal pornography, narcotics and firearms. You can even find an online 'Assassination Market', where people pay to have their enemies murdered. Bartlett observed a Gomorrah-like mall of unlimited horrors. Nevertheless, the dark web hints at the kind of cash libertarianism Hayek and his followers proselytized. It represents 'an underworld set apart yet connected to the internet we inhabit, a world of complete freedom and anonymity, and where users say and do what they like, often uncensored and unregulated . . . it's dark because we rarely see it: it tends to be hidden, obscure and secret'.[36]

The dark net is cash-individualism gone wild, and another Hayekian venture into the economy of sleaze. What if Karl Marx was correct when he said that the capitalist profit motive is not simply a matter of unbridled greed (too much humanity of an ugly kind) but the formation of an existential *lack* that ultimately hollows out who we are? Under capitalism more generally, according to Marx, money hatches inner demons that separate us from our potential, instigating 'the overturning of all human and natural qualities, the fraternization of impossibilities – the *divine* power of money lies in its *character* as men's estranged, alienating and self-disposing species-nature. Money is the *alienated ability of mankind.'*[37] If so, then things get truly creepy when we are confronted with the dark net and its atrocious version of our species being. We're not only dealing with man's alienated abilities but also his unconscious *inabilities*, what he *cannot* do without the cover of the dark net. Survival of the fittest? No, more like survival of the filthiest.

Entrepreneurial Death Drive

Hayek might have remained an obscure figure if it wasn't for Milton Friedman. He had joined Chicago University in the 1940s, and his 1962 book *Capitalism and Freedom* made him famous.[38] It was widely read as the US version of Hayek's *The Road to Serfdom*. In the 1970s and 1980s, Friedman embarked on a gruelling lecture series to spread the free market faith, appearing on popular talk shows (such as *Donahue*) and speaking on campuses across America. In 1980, he even got his own TV show, *Free to Choose*. Here he gives even the most contentious assertion in Hayek's *The Road to Serfdom* a kind of folksy common-sense credibility. Each episode tackles the ingrained collectivism (and even semi-socialism) of the American mind, trying to convince people that government is a threat to their individual liberty.

Episode 8 of *Free to Choose* deals with workers' rights and radiates the New Right's hatred of the labour movement. When it comes to an open and free labour market, Friedman argues, there should be absolutely no entry barriers to jobs and occupations in the economy. This is especially so if workers try to increase the security of jobs by restricting access to them, a time-honoured strategy for protecting pay and conditions. Here Friedman is rehearsing – almost verbatim – an argument developed by Hayek some thirty-five years earlier:

if the producer, be he an entrepreneur or worker, is to be protected against underbidding from outsiders, it means that others
who are worse off are precluded from sharing in the relatively
greater prosperity of the controlled industries. Every restriction
on the freedom of entry into trade reduces the security of all
those outside it.[39]

In this episode of *Free to Choose*, the main 'restrictions' Friedman has
in mind here are those erected by his old foe: trade unions and professional associations of various kinds that seek to safeguard the skills,
status and wages of workers.

In making this argument, Friedman had his work cut out for him.
Post-war capitalism in America was built upon strong trade unions
and powerful professional bodies. So he begins the episode on the
sunny Greek island of Kos, where one of the founders of modern medicine, Hippocrates, set up a school in the fourth century BC. Friedman
explains how students established the Hippocratic Oath after their
master died. A particular clause is read to viewers: 'I will impart a
knowledge of the art to my own self and those of my teachers and
to disciples bound by a stipulation and oath according to the law of
medicine, but to none others.'[40] Today we would call that a closed
shop, Friedman swiftly says with scorn.

Another passage from the oath is recited, this time concerning painful kidney stones: 'I will not cut persons labouring under the stone but
will leave this to be done by men who are practitioners of this work.'
Friedman smirks: don't we have here a nice market-sharing agreement
between physicians and surgeons?

For Friedman, this is a terrible situation, of course, and he believes
Hippocrates would have disapproved too. Anyone ought to be able to
provide medical care if they have the expertise and a customer willing

to pay. It's at this point that Friedman goes after his real target with characteristic alacrity:

> He would strongly have objected to the kind of restrictive practices that physicians all over the world have adopted to protect their custom. In the United States the American Medical Association has for decades been one of the strongest labor unions in the country, keeping down the number of physicians, keeping up the costs of medical care, preventing competition by people from outside the profession with those in it. All, of course, in the name of helping the patient. Without warning, any one of us may suddenly need medical care. If we do, we want the very best care we can get. But who can give us that care? Is it always a graduate of an expensive medical school who has a union card called a medical license? Or might it be someone like this: a trained paramedic working for a private enterprise organization rendering emergency care? Why should medical care be a monopoly of licensed physicians? Shouldn't anyone who is capable of providing effective help be free to do so?[41]

The show now cuts to modern California, where private paramedics are tending to an ill patient. Anyone who has visited the USA understands the militant obsession it has with medicine and longevity. So Friedman's chosen his topic matter prudently. He interviews a paramedic who claims that his team is much more responsive to emergency call-outs than mainstream providers. That's what the American Medical Association simply don't understand: 'they take the Hippocratic Oath here in the United States and they believe that they should be the one that is treating their patient. They should be the one that saves that patient's life. And if someone else does it, it just kind of interferes with everything that they have been taught.'[42]

Friedman's message is simple. In an open and free market, a single group of experts – say, oncologists or medieval historians – shouldn't monopolize practice on these subjects. Others should have a voice too, including you and I. Friedman believed that professional associations and the credentialism they promote are simply a ruse to bolster workers' power – artificially pushing up the market price and shutting alternative providers out of the occupation. In the end, it's the critically ill patient waiting for an ambulance who is the real loser.

Perhaps we now finally get to the central theme of this *Free to Choose* episode: unions kill! The paranoid bluster about entry barriers hurting other workers and the self-seeking inclinations of certified professionals is really a convenient excuse for undermining large unions. The American Medical Association and the American Labour Federation Friedman despised the most. Moreover, no doubt his arguments would help Ronald Reagan's victory over the Air Traffic Controllers' union in 1981. Breaking up this organization was a significant blow to the workers' movement not only in the USA, but in the Western world more widely.[43]

Dirty Experts

Hayek and Friedman disagreed on the finer details of neoclassical economics. But when it came to Hayek's utopian image of market individualism, Friedman became a devout follower – particularly in relation to work and occupations.[44] And, as Friedman's arguments found a sympathetic audience among policy-makers in the 1980s, a path slowly cleared for the rapid deformalization we see today. Three steps are important.

Firstly, we can observe the attempt to *decollectivize* the worker in these arguments, to transform a homogeneous workforce into self-contained individuals who compete in an open labour market. Concepts like 'human capital' (developed by T. W. Schultz and Gary Becker) had this very purpose in mind, because it counteracted the labour-centric discourse of socialism, both outside and inside the USA.[45]

Once work is isolated and privatized in this manner, a second step occurs, which intends to remove another 'entrance barrier' to certain occupations – credentials and qualifications. It is interesting that Friedman focuses on medicine in order to demonstrate how licensing distorts an open labour market. His arguments are outlandish, of course. He's on the verge of promoting quackery, which the profession spent years trying to banish given the mortal dangers (and exploitation) that it precipitated. For Friedman, anyone should be able to sell medical care and advice (or sex work, taxi services, education, etc.) if there is someone willing to purchase it. If it transpires that their service is negligent, they'll soon go out of business as patients gravitate to safer competitors or use tort laws to gain recompense (Friedman doesn't seem to care that a few consumers might be seriously harmed along the way, as his comments about Thalidomide indicate).[46] Libertarian jurist Richard Epstein takes the argument even further, suggesting that malpractice law ought to be limited in this area, too. Instead, physicians and patients can negotiate 'private agreements' about liability in the advent of professional misconduct.[47]

At any rate, we can connect this attack on licensing to the wider trend of occupational deprofessionalization, which resonates with Hayek's contention in *The Road to Serfdom* that anyone ought to be free to sell anything in an open society. Deprofessionalization is particularly evident in the UK, perhaps due to Thatcher's staunch admiration for Hayek and the longstanding influence of her ideas even today. For example, to become a taxi-driver in London, drivers once required a good deal of training and regulatory input.[48] Uber did away with that, of course. Or take the example of policing. Law enforcement officials have long treated vigilante groups with considerable suspicion for obvious reasons. But that's changing too. Police investigators now co-operate with unauthorized 'paedophile hunters' (who pose as children online and then arrange a meeting), using their evidence to gain convictions.[49] Permutations are under way in regular policing roles too, with Police Community Support Officers (PCSOs) increasingly important. They receive much less training than ordinary officers and are not permitted to join the Police Federation union. No closed shop here. The scheme has not been without controversy. In 2007, it was discovered that Thames Valley Police Force had mistakenly recruited sixteen- and seventeen-year-olds as PCSOs.[50]

What about education? In England, the Conservative government pioneered so-called 'free schools'. They do not fall under the control of local authorities and often form corporate partnerships, which inevitably influences the curriculum. These schools are controversial because teachers don't require any formal training or gain Qualified Teacher Status (QTS). Politicians claimed this would promote 'innovation, diversity and flexibility'.[51] One newspaper columnist lampooned the initiative and followed some of its implications: 'surely the Government must extend this method to other workplaces, such as operating theatres and nuclear submarines. The Royal Navy could [insist] there are plenty of excellent candidates who could command a nuclear sub, having fired torpedoes on Modern Warfare 2, but they're put off by the red tape of having to prove they're "qualified", leaving our coast unprotected.'[52]

The scene is now set for the third and final step towards deformalization – undermining the skilled expertise of trained officials. Take the now infamous Brexit referendum in 2016. When Vote

Leave campaigners claimed that EU membership cost Britain £350 million a week, the figure was deemed 'potentially misleading' by the UK Statistical Society because it omitted the EU rebate. The Institute of Fiscal Studies also raised concerns. In response to these criticisms, a prominent member of the Leave campaign famously stated that the British people had had enough of experts.[53]

In the USA, Donald Trump supporters launched a similar attack on the 'expertariat', a term coined by climate change denier Myron Ebell to discredit scientists working on global warming.[54] Amazingly enough, Trump appointed him to lead the transition team for the United States Environmental Protection Agency (EPA). Indeed, Trump's version of 'corporate populism' actively encourages the use of 'alternative facts', whereby ordinary people feel empowered to replace experts and do a better job.[55] The relativism of values/knowledge that Hayek thought was fundamental to the free market reaches its sad conclusion at this point . . . in 2016 the *Oxford English Dictionary* announced its word of the year: *post-truth*. In the age of Sugar Daddy capitalism, everything is for sale to the highest bidder, even *truth* itself – now generated by Russian social media bots.

Chapter Three

Wiki-feudalism

The Grenfell Tower fire in London shocked the world in June 2017. Disasters like this weren't supposed to happen in this day and age. The blaze was started by a fridge-freezer in a fourth-floor flat around 1 a.m. By the time the first squad of firefighters arrived, the inferno had spread. External cladding on the tower was blamed. It was highly flammable. At least eighty people died in the fire, including children and families. Some residents had leaped to their death from windows, hoping to escape the blanket of thick black smoke by any means possible. Others hopelessly cried for help in their kitchens, waving arms and turning lights on and off to gain attention. Perhaps the most heart-breaking revelation concerned the fate of six-month-old Leena Belkadi.[1] An inquest found she died in her mother's arms from smoke inhalation in a stairwell between the nineteenth and twentieth floors.

How could such a horrible catastrophe occur in one of the richest countries in the world? Grenfell Tower was primarily 'council' or public housing. The 129 flats mainly accommodated working-class residents. The block fell under the authority of the Royal Borough of Kensington and Chelsea and was maintained by management firm KCTMO (Kensington & Chelsea Tenant Management Organisation). A major renovation of Grenfell was completed in 2016. Investigators learnt that KCTMO had dropped the original contractors – Leadbitter – because they couldn't keep within the council's strict budget.[2] Rival company

Rydon was awarded the job instead.[3] In order to save around £300,000, a fire-resistant cladding was replaced with a cheaper version, which was banned on tall buildings in the USA and Germany, given its flammable qualities.[4] After a similar London fire had occurred at Shepherd's Court in 2016, an insurance firm declared that the cladding caused 'extremely rapid fire spread and the release of large volumes of toxic smoke . . . This allows extensive and violent fire to spread, and makes firefighting almost impossible.'[5] The London Fire Brigade repeatedly raised concerns about it being used in housing blocks like Grenfell.[6]

Other avoidable factors were behind the tragic fire. The Grenfell Tower Leaseholders' Association had complained about fire safety long before that fateful night. The day after the blaze, a spokesperson said 'all our warnings fell on deaf ears and we predicted that a catastrophe like this was inevitable and just a matter of time'.[7] There wasn't a sprinkler system in place. Fire extinguishers were out of date and had 'condemned' signs on them. No fire instructions were posted and the building's wiring was viewed with deep suspicion by occupants. Residents were also worried about having only one staircase for an emergency exit. Two are mandatory in other countries, for obvious reasons. London Mayor Sadiq Khan was critical of the advice KCTMO had given residents.[8] In the event of a fire, stay put and do not evacuate. They believed that fires would be contained within a single apartment. Moreover, the last fire inspection took place in 2015.[9] Regulations stipulate that risk assessment be performed following any material change to a building of this sort. But it isn't specified exactly *when* this should occur. The government's funding of the fire services didn't help either. Inspectors specializing in high-rise buildings lost 244 officers between 2011 and 2017.[10] Overall, funding to fire services had been slashed by up to 39 per cent during the same period.[11]

Architectures of Fire

While cost-cutting and neglect were undoubtedly contributing factors to the Grenfell tragedy, I think it was also connected to the effort to debureaucratize, deregulate, and what I call *deformalize* the economy in the UK. When the question of central sprinklers was broached in parliament back in 2014, for example, the then Housing Minister brashly stated:

> Under that rule, when the Government introduce a regulation, we will identify two existing ones to be removed. The Department for Communities and Local Government has gone further and removed an even higher proportion of regulations. In that context, Members will understand why we want to exhaust all non-regulatory options before we introduce any new regulations.[12]

He went on to say: 'there are always calls for Government to change building regulations, and that is often the default position of those who see regulation as an easy answer . . . however, it is not the only answer. We should intervene only if it is entirely necessary, and only as a last resort. The cost of fitting a fire sprinkler system may affect house building – something we want to encourage.' Since regulations were being stripped back in this manner, it was up to individual 'housing providers and building owners to make informed decisions about the fire safety measures that are appropriate for their circumstances'.

Neoclassical or neoliberal governance policies have been steadily deregulating certain sectors of the UK. Until the mid-1980s, the London Buildings Act required high-rise exteriors to have at least one hour's fire resistance.[13] These laws can be traced back to Christopher Wren's recommendations following the 1666 Great Fire of London.

When Margaret Thatcher came into power, these old rules were considered useless red tape and replaced in 1986 by the National Buildings Regulations.[14] The stipulation that materials in these structures must be non-combustible was dropped.

The Tory Coalition government led by Prime Minister David Cameron took this anti-regulation drive very seriously indeed.[15] In 2011, the Red Tape Challenge was founded. Its goal was to reduce regulation and encourage independent business and enterprise.[16] In a 2014 speech to the Federation of Small Businesses, Cameron spoke of the vigour with which he planned to rid England of red tape: 'We will be the first government in modern history to have reduced – rather than increased – domestic business regulation during our time in office.'[17] Particularly notable in the speech was his focus on safety regulations: 'This government has already stopped needless health and safety inspections . . . And the new Deregulation Bill will exempt 1 million self-employed people from health and safety law altogether.' In light of the 2017 London acid attacks on random pedestrians, the following statement in the same speech is particularly disconcerting: 'Shopkeepers used to need a poison licence to sell oven cleaner – we're scrapping that.'

Whereas Cameron happily dubbed his initiative the Red Tape Challenge, in 2014 one astute commentator evoked a different phrase that proved prophetic . . . 'bonfire of the building regulations'.[18] The concept of a Red Tape Challenge was devised by one-time Cameron advisor and friend, Steve Hilton.[19] He was also the brains behind the 'Big Society' ideology that was launched in 2010 to much fanfare. Hardly anyone understood what it meant. But proponents said it was designed to encourage economic decentralization, localism in the community and volunteering. This basically made it a replica of the 'small government' idea (with the noun 'big' added as a British

Orwellian touch) that's been popular in the USA for many years. When forced to explain once more what 'Big Society' looked like in practice, David Cameron said, 'There's one word at the heart of all this, and that is responsibility. We need people to take more responsibility. We need people to act more responsibly, because if you take any problem in our country and you just think: "Well, what can the government do to sort it out?", that is only ever going to be half of the answer.'[20] Critics simply saw the concept of Big Society as a thinly veiled excuse to cut public spending and let large organizations regulate (or *not*, in the case of Grenfell) themselves.

Computer Says 'No'

Steve Hilton was Cameron's 'blue sky' policy advisor (a.k.a. 'guru') until he departed for California to start his own business in 2012. Today, he hosts a Trump-friendly news show on the Fox Network that celebrates 'positive populism' and includes segments called 'Swamp Watch'. During his time at No. 10 Downing Street, it was said that Hilton would wander the building wearing a T-shirt, shorts and socks as he dreamed up new ideas. His casual appearance was probably an attempt to funk up the Tory Party image. According to one government insider, Hilton's eccentric views were tolerated, but only up to a point: 'regulation stood for everything Steve loathed and misunderstood in government. Every past attempt to hack it away having failed, a classic Hilton idea was born. All 21,000 would be put online, and through the wisdom of crowds the public would root out and elect the worst for destruction.'[21]

In 2011, some of Hilton's more questionable suggestions for jump-starting the economy were leaked to the press. They included the advantages of scrapping maternity leave and all consumer protection law 'to see what would happen'.[22] To deal with unemployment, Jobcentres would be closed and community groups set up instead.[23] In sum, and to reiterate a neoclassical motif now all-too familiar in the Anglo-American world, government is part of the problem, not the solution.

Hilton's politics is outlined in his best-selling book *More Human*.[24] The idea is simple. Mammoth bureaucracies have slowly taken over society, with all but the very rich feeling as if they're nothing more than a number. Distant and robotic officials manage these large organizations in the energy, health and education sectors, and have little accountability to average citizens. Because bureaucrats are generally self-serving and detached from the people they preside over, it's easy for these faceless organizations to act inhumanely. According to Hilton, examples of dehumanization are everywhere around us. Passengers are unceremoniously thrown off planes because airlines have little concern for individual customers. How could they, given the millions they transport? The unemployed are treated like second-class citizens. Children are processed in 'factory schools'. The food industry churns out substandard produce controlled by monolithic supermarket chains who are destroying our health as they make millions. Hospitals are more concerned with paperwork and performance measures than individual patients languishing in uncaring settings. And business firms see employees as replaceable 'resources'. An inevitable corollary of these overblown organizations is the proliferation of useless rules and regulations, many of which have not been designed with a unique, living end-user in mind (i.e., an actual human being).

Hilton certainly is no fan of government nor its propensity to crowd out entrepreneurs and drown the population in red tape. But he also directs a good deal of criticism at giant corporations too, which have created private monopolies to exploit consumers/workers with impunity in many sectors. He believes that these private monopolies undermine the philosophy of competitive enterprise, a sentiment he shares with Chicago School economists. However, advocates of free market capitalism – such as Hilton – forget the important role that the Chicago School of Law played in justifying the emergence of private monopolies.[25] Aaron Director, for example, worked relentlessly to counter the anti-trust bias of neoclassical economics and significantly influenced academics in the economics department in the process.[26] A new perspective began to crystallize back in the 1960s. Corporate monopolies (resulting from vertical integration, interlocking directorates, mergers and so forth) are still preferable to state-owned organizations if they efficiently allocate resources, despite their singular control over an industry. Milton Friedman and others like Richard Posner and Thomas Sowell soon saw the light too: it's only when private monopolies are *coercive* that they cause trouble in terms of price gouging, workers' rights, consumer safety, etc.

The logic was a sham, of course, and the language wasn't so friendly when it came to state monopolies or trade unions. The position reveals how stubbornly pro-capitalist some of these early neoliberal thinkers were. Indeed, I cannot think of one corporate monopoly that has refrained from automatically exploiting its position in some manner. Moreover, what you and I as workers/consumers view as plainly *coercive* can just as easily be interpreted as fair by politicians besotted by the mythos of private enterprise. It's in this way that so many governments in the 1980s and 1990s got away with privatizing public services (water supply, transport, mail, etc.), even those that could never face proper competition in the Hayekian sense. The long-term outcome has been bad for workers, not only in rising commodity prices. The concentration of capital in the USA, for example, has been linked to a decline in the labour share of income and stagnating wages. That's because the pool of employers has shrunk (tending towards a monopsony, or one buyer of labour power interacting with many sellers), thus undermining worker bargaining power since they have fewer alternative job options in any given sector.[27]

Hospice Nation

For Hilton, the problem with most bureaucracies in both public and private sectors is mainly one of *size*: 'too often the people making decisions are too far removed from the people affected by them. How can policy-makers (most of whom are holed in London and other administrative centres) possibly achieve such a nuanced awareness of people in communities around the country?'[28] He wants organizations to scale down dramatically, be more responsive to local needs . . . closer to real people and their communities. A number of examples are presented in which local organizations provide goods and services of a superior quality compared to gargantuan bureaucracies. But it's easy for the reader of *More Human* to conclude that perhaps it is organizations *in general* – collective institutions that are more than the sum of their individual parts – that Hilton sees as the enemy. They have a bad habit of growing, forming an authoritarian elite and depersonalizing its members and clients.

Big organizations are more interested in self-perpetuation than achieving meaningful goals. They thereby thrive on rules, regulations and red tape in order to remain consistent across a broad spectrum of peoples. Hilton hates all of this. He surmises: 'the most human possible scale is that of individual people and their families'.[29] As opposed to big bureaucracy, a 'big society' follows very different principles that decentre power and governance. Individuals take responsibility for their own welfare, and develop agile and authentic local networks to provide care, food, education and healthcare for those closest to them. The state and its technocratic fiefdoms could never achieve the receptiveness that grassroots networks do.

As Hilton develops his argument, his economic agenda becomes apparent. As with his big society concept, this 'more human' localism is really about helping to roll back public spending. For example, Hilton laments how public hospitals in the UK waste so many resources on end-of-life care for terminally ill patients. If we gave them the freedom to choose, he suggests, most would prefer to die at home tended by loved ones (Hilton doesn't tell us how the families of these care-intensive patients might feel about replacing a trained palliative carer). Freeing up hospital beds will save taxpayers a sizeable amount of cash and also liberate the terminally ill.

A number of very telling shifts in logic occur at this point in Hilton's manifesto. We might well believe that the qualities that make us 'human' are too diverse and historically conditioned to define in any certain manner. But Hilton does so with brio. Humans display a great individual appetite for commerce. Whether we know it or not, we're all intrinsically businesspeople, which is why free market enterprise should be unleashed and an ultra-decentralized system established. For 'the notion of the entrepreneur, the calling of enterprise, is profoundly human'.[30] The anti-organizational flavour of Hilton's argument becomes a rallying call for monetary individualism or 'anarcho-capitalism', whereby we all become our own bosses, dedicated human capitalists who do as we please.

Attempting to realize this utopian dream has landed Hilton in trouble. In 2008, he was arrested by the Transport Police after a dispute about his train ticket.[31] And in 2011, it was leaked that Hilton asked government officials why exactly the Prime Minister had to obey the law ... because he would go to jail, a weary advisor responded.[32] As all good libertarians believe, the law ought to be distrusted, especially if it suffocates the entrepreneur within. In his book, Hilton implies that anti-social behaviour stems from the very regulations designed to curb it. He cites an experiment by Robert Cialdini in the USA.[33] The Petrified Forest National Park in Arizona has a longstanding problem with visitors pilfering the ancient wood. On a hunch, Cialdini erected signs reminding visitors that this is strictly prohibited. Weirdly, locations in the park where the signs stood saw an increase in theft. What was going on? For Cialdini, the formal warning inadvertently signalled to people that taking wood was in fact a norm. The underlying message here is obvious. Governmental rules and laws don't work. And isn't that something all multinational senior executives would love to hear?

The Birth of Wiki-feudalism

Hilton's narrative starts to key into the ideological currents that are now reshaping our society significantly – mostly for the worst, I suggest.

Firstly, in this individualized, ruleless (and imaginary) capitalist environment, technology rather than big bureaucracy is what helps us become more human. Take the National Health Service (NHS). According to Hilton, the best way to promote quality healthcare in the UK is to reduce the size of the institutions involved. The NHS dominates the sector. It needs to be broken up into a 'new marketplace for healthcare services, where many different providers compete for patients on a level playing field'.[34] Patient responsiveness can be assisted by information technologies. Telemedicine will allow doctors to perform services online. A firm called Healthtap in the USA, for example, lets users post questions for doctors to answer without having to visit a consultation room. In the UK, firms like 'Push Doctor' provide GP consultations for a fee. According to Hilton, 'technology can be harnessed to put healthcare in the hands of the patient through medical apps and social networks'.[35]

And then comes the second motif. Coexisting with this Californian ideology of high-tech individualism is the yearning to return to a less complex, pre-industrial age. The birth of monster bureaucracies only occurred when industrial society fully committed to the modernist project, in Western countries at least. Underlying all the talk about digital capitalism is a nostalgia for a 'simpler' world before the modern state took over and messed things up: 'before the industrial revolution, politics, government and business were almost entirely local – because they had to be. Rulers simply did not have the information and reach to make decisions about individual people's lives or run centralized bureaucracies. Local government or feudal lords were delegated almost all sovereign power, answering only nominally to far-off capital . . . this period we could call the pre-bureaucratic age'.[36]

Hilton is best seen as a proponent of second-wave neoliberalism. The first wave (represented by F. A. Hayek and Friedman, as discussed in previous chapters) aimed to filter all social life through the price mechanism. It was thought that this would anonymize everyone, but it inadvertently hastened deformalization as the state and public sphere withdrew. Second-wave neoliberalism tries to paste a human face on these business activities, particularly celebrating the informal domain. Hilton's 'more human' narrative, therefore, is an attempt to overlay the monetary formalism of market individualism (the lone entrepreneur, self-employed contractor, etc.) onto the patrimonial qualities of a pre-modern social order. The result is a kind of *wiki-feudalism*, in which personal connections come to the fore in determining whether you sink or swim. In an era defined by 'extreme neoliberalism', families and networks are suddenly paramount.[37] Not the law or due process. And certainly not the state and its public institutions.

Wiki-feudalism adheres to contradictory social logics. First, the only interactions that really matter are financial ones. They are freely entered into and supposedly empower the individual. A younger person seeking to move up the social hierarchy might obtain a student loan. A retired plumber who is short of cash might set up as a self-employed contractor, and so forth. And second, the mobility and choice that are meant to derive from individual market transactions turn into the opposite: a deeply unfree situation. Student debt becomes a kind of never-ending bondage. A worker hired as an independent contractor discovers that they're really *de facto* employees with zero rights and unable to find work elsewhere.

These two logics represent a major tension at the centre of neoliberal society, ceaselessly unsettling the rhetoric of personal freedom and click-democracy that currently pervades the dominant views about how the economy functions. Add to this the celebration of pre-bureaucratic informalism – everyone doing 'deals', to use the parlance of Donald Trump – then we enter the space of an (albeit futuristic) economic dark age. What were once official and potentially transparent power relationships (between labour and capital, for example) now draw upon informal arrangements as well. While this may look civil and 'more human' on the surface, unchecked authority has a nasty habit of acting deeply irrationally without notice, like dining with Caligula.

When we add undue influence and control into the mix, Steve Hilton's right-wing dream of individual entrepreneurs is now looking more like something out of *The Godfather*. Indeed, in true feudalist fashion, the mafia is an apt simile, given its lawlessness, emphasis on strong personal ties in business, and unpredictable callousness when a deal goes bad. No wonder organized crime syndicates love neoliberal capitalism so much![38] The bonfire of regulations and the minimal state intervention have provided a veritable bonanza for the criminal black market, which has penetrated the global flows of goods and services on an unprecedented level.

Bureau Inferno

The adoration of IT solutions to redress the grave flaws of neoliberal capitalism disguises the regressive reality unfolding before us in the age of wiki-feudalism. Individual-based 'click humanism' is revered by libertarian capitalists today since it's seen to epitomize all that bureaucracy isn't. But why this hatred of bureaucracy in the first place?

Bureaucracy has been around since ancient China and the Roman Empire. But the modern version of it we recognize today emerged in eighteenth- and early nineteenth-century France, Prussia and Britain. From the beginning it's been viewed with both awe and horror. Civil servants coolly reigning over paperwork and files (usually for purposes of taxation and trade) in large, impersonal organizations provided an incomparable source of power to the state. And bureaucracy has an uncanny ability to replicate, expand and grow, almost of its own accord. For example, in the USA, these types of organizations built the giant railroads that modernized the country in the mid nineteenth century, but also spawned the archetypical 'salaried manager' who soon controlled massive organizations in both the public and private sectors. As business historian Alfred Chandler put it, the fabled 'invisible hand' of the American free market system (the pre-1850 'Wild West') was swiftly replaced by the 'visible hand' of private conglomerates. It has pretty much stayed that way ever since with large multinationals ruling the economy.[39]

German sociologist Max Weber provided one of the earliest and most enduring criticisms of modern bureaucracy.[40] He too was impressed by what it could achieve. Observance of tradition and superstition had clouded the minds of organizers for millennia in what Weber called 'prebendal' arrangements (which follow custom and patronage) – but not the modern bureaucrat. He or she is totally calculating, ultra-rational and able to store records and plan like no one else: precise, fast, unambiguous, and lacking sentimentalism. *Formalism* was key to bureaucracy's early successes and subsequent spread, according to Weber. In the modern office, there's no place for love, passion, fear or hate. The private feelings or personal background of the bureaucrat are of little consequence when a bureaucracy is functioning properly. The official dispassionately dispatches their business in a uniform manner, soberly following clear rules and regulations. It's because of their expertise/training that they hold office, not family connections or patrimony. Weber saw this as the upside. But there was a downside too. A world managed by the bureaucratic mind is certainly reasonable, but also profoundly soulless. In Weber's terminology, life becomes 'disenchanted' as a result and bereft of the human qualities that make it worth living.

This criticism of modern organizations opened the floodgates in terms of tarnishing the reputation of bureaucracy. Two camps emerged – namely, those from the political left and those on the right. Left-leaning critics see in bureaucracy a powerful tool for unfairly dominating the population, particularly in relation to the class structure that underpins capitalist society. US sociologists such as Alvin Gouldner and C. Wright Mills (who translated a number of Weber's key texts) noted the tyrannical tendencies of administration in 1950s

America.[41] Not only do bureaucrats mindlessly police rules for their own sake, but manage institutions that can be repressive and anti-democratic. The radical Marxist Herbert Marcuse struck a chord in the 1960s with this criticism. His book *One-Dimensional Man* revealed how modern rationality had become a sort of psychic prison that turns the masses into docile conformists with no imagination or fire.[42] The book was a wild success since it appeared just as the counter-culture was under way. Kids were rejecting the staid conformity of their parents, dropping acid and zoning out to *Are You Experienced.* Bureaucratic reason once promised to liberate us from the barbarism of premodern life. And it partially did. But the price was a drone-like existence and never-ending surveillance: 'a comfortable, smooth, reasonable, demo-cratic unfreedom prevails in advanced civilization, a token of technical progress'.[43]

Radical priest Ivan Illich takes the argument even further. He became an intellectual celebrity after publishing *Deschooling Society* in the early 1970s. Modern schools were described as a variation of the automobile factory or meat-processing plant.[44] Their main purpose was to produce standardized students and starve them of alternative skills and ways of being. According to Illich, big bureaucracies are dan-gerous for this very reason . . . they kill all other forms of knowledge. When functionaries run our healthcare and education, for example, they not only monopolize know-how but also shut down local methods of mutual aid in the name of science. Civic groups, family units and individuals are rendered impotent, passive and unable to help them-selves. The 'expertariat' naturally expand in numbers and influence because the forces of normalization are always seeking new domains of conquest. Illich lays much of the blame on the size and scale of these institutions: 'When an enterprise [or an institution] grows beyond a certain point on this scale, it first frustrates the end for which it was originally designed, and then rapidly becomes a threat to society itself.'[45]

The Dystopia of Rules

Criticisms of bureaucracy from the right of the political spectrum are now familiar – specifically, the views of Hayek and Friedman. Two themes are worth noting.

First, neoclassical economists believe that human liberty depends on individual financial self-reliance, first and foremost. According to Hayek, behind all those rather romantic and grandiose demands for 'social justice' on the political left is in fact a rather sober and unromantic reality when it comes to securing freedom – namely, *cash*: 'money is one of the greatest instruments for freedom ever invented by man'.[46] Monetarized market individualism, rather than 'politics', will deliver the freest society for all. That's because government bureaucrats and central planners invariably lose touch with distinct individuals and their unique preferences. Planners cannot help but take a broad, bird's - eye view of society since they are dealing with large groups. A remote and spreadsheet-like survey of *mass society* is required in government, which leads to 'one-size-fits-all' programmes because they're easier for bureaucrats to administer compared to costly, individually tailored policies.

Hayek's opposition to state bureaucracy and central planning also has a more technical side. No single institution can collect, process and manage all the information circulating in the economy. The pricing mechanism in an unregulated market can do this, however, making it infinitely more sensitive to individual agency. It dispenses with the need for overarching governance structures and coordination. Free from red tape and restrictions, the invisible hand of the price system starts to resemble the characteristics of Wikipedia in Hayek's analysis, albeit a highly capitalist version of the open-access online encyclopaedia: 'the mere fact that there is one price for any commodity . . . brings about the solution which might have been arrived at by one single mind possessing all the information which is in fact dispersed among all the people involved in the process.'[47]

The second criticism of bureaucracy focuses on government regulators and can be found in a branch of neoclassical economics called Public Choice Theory. It rose to prominence in the 1980s and is associated with academics such as James M. Buchanan and William A. Niskanen.[48] They found Weber's picture of state bureaucrats – as disinterested officials – too naïve. Buchanan said he instead preferred a theory of government that dropped the romance: 'politicians and bureaucrats are no different from the rest of us. They will maximize their incentives just like everybody else.'[49] This sentiment chimes more with the cynical views of Weber's pupil, Robert Michels, who claimed that *all organizations*, no matter how democratic and in touch with their members to begin with, end up with an unaccountable, oligarchic class at their apex (it's not surprising that Michels later joined Mussolini's fascist party).[50] Similarly, public choice scholars refused to see civil servants as objective functionaries: Weber was wrong. They have agendas of their own and vie for power. Rather than serving the public, self-preservation and resource hoarding are their chief objectives. Moreover, state institutions tend to engage in 'rent-seeking' behaviour in the economy, asserting their monopolistic predominance by controlling access to public resources.

As David Graeber explains in his excellent critique of bureaucracy – *The Utopia of Rules* – it feels as if pointless paperwork has truly won the day. It's everywhere. However, I suggest that this is not simply a problem with the state-form. Free market politicians and mainstream economists would have us believe that we're drowning in governmental red tape, but that is not necessarily true. So-called 'big government' still exists in relation to the defence budget and bank bail-outs – but community-orientated public services? In the UK at least, this part of the state has drastically shrunk over the last ten years.[51] Sure, the *coercive state* has increased its dominion over the middle classes and working poor, but mostly disappeared for the rich. Whereas generous welfare programmes have been a boon for the corporate class – yet evaporated for everyone else.

Salmonella Nights

Take the funding system of local authorities and councils in the UK.[52] The rich often don't need these institutions, but the rest of us do. Politicians told us that they were devolving power, putting it back in the hands of locals so that services could become more agile and strategic. The idea clearly fits with Hilton's more human philosophy, in more ways than one. At the same time as power was devolved, the councils were given much less cash. Make do with that, they were told – a poisoned chalice if ever there was one. As pointed out in a depressing article by Tom Crewe, 'no other area of government has been subject to the same squeeze: since the start of the decade, spending by local authorities has been reduced by 37 per cent, and is scheduled to fall much further over the next five years. For many councils this will mean the loss of more than 60 per cent of their income by 2020.'[53]

This means fewer libraries, public toilets and parks, and reduced care for the elderly. It also means more indebtedness since, as a general rule, any reduction of public spending increases private debt among ordinary members of society, a trend that could conclude with another major financial meltdown according to some analysts. Regardless, it appears to be regulatory bodies – the 'red tape' everybody loves to hate – that've been hit the hardest. We already know what has happened to the fire service. Because there are fewer trained inspectors, 45 per cent fewer enforcement notices were issued between 2010 and 2017. In some districts, fire safety audits dropped by 66 per cent over the same period.[54] Or take environmental health officers. They're employed by the council to monitor the food we consume and check it's safe and accurately labelled. Officers also examine residential building safety, a sector of the economy that's been relatively under-regulated in cities like London where a kind of predatory ethos prevails among landlords. We ought to express our gratefulness to environmental protection officers like these. Who knows what we might end up eating or what death-traps might be rented out to us without them. However, funding to these agencies has been radically cut. As a result, food hygiene inspections, for example, have fallen by 15 per cent since 2003.[55] According to the Food Standards Agency, almost 47,000 fewer inspections were carried out in 2014 than in 2003. And the number of restaurants and cafés prosecuted fell by 35 per cent, from 552 to 361 over the same period.[56]

It is no surprise that food poisoning is a problem in England. According to the Centre for Crime and Justice Studies, each year avoidable food contamination kills 500 people and hospitalizes 200,000.[57] A spokesperson described what 'unregulated Britain' really means: 'this is not about rules, regulations and red tape. It is about lives lost and the health of communities, workers and consumers made poorer. This is avoidable business-generated, state-facilitated social murder. And quite remarkably it proceeds daily, met largely by political silence.'[58] Not quite the caring human world that Hilton imagined, if only meddling bureaucracies were swept away.

The fact of the matter is this. The state – especially when it comes to upholding the values of the *public sphere* – is already anaemic in many parts of society. The punitive arm of government and its war machine appears to be the only growth area where funding is concerned. Moreover, life governed by the system of unregulated and hyper-individualized enterprise that Hilton idealizes (along with Hayek, Friedman and Boris Johnson) is frequently not a pretty one in reality. Sure, it involves some very human qualities . . . such as diarrhoea and projectile vomiting after an outbreak of salmonella poisoning. But no doubt there will soon be a neat app available (developed by a California start-up perhaps) that will be able to track the virus as it works its way through your body. This is wiki-feudalism in action.

Individuals (like you and I) often regulate themselves when it comes to observing community rules and norms. Society would swiftly fall apart otherwise. However, the cult of 'self-regulation' is seldom effective for profit-making enterprises because the temptation to cut corners and screw consumers, workers and/or the natural environment is often too strong. That's not because the people who run them are morally 'bad'. But if the objective is to maximize surpluses, no matter what, then a kind of *external* limit is required, imposed from the outside, preferably by the public if possible. Otherwise, anything can happen. It's these very limits that have been relaxed under neoliberal capitalism and now the chickens are coming home to roost – hence the recent scandals around food safety and hygiene. A US report found that pig and chicken plants consistently violate food hygiene standards, some in ways too disgusting to relay here.[59] Let's put this in context. The US Centers for Disease Control and Prevention estimates that 48 million Americans contract foodborne illnesses every year, with a significant number of hospitalizations and deaths involved.[60]

Home Office Hell

Scale is not the problem with bureaucracy. When it comes to civic works – such as fire safety or food hygiene – the bigger the better, I would argue. Could market individualism ever have matched the great achievements of bureaucracy in this respect? Vaccination? The postal service? Transport and public health? I don't think so, because it's the *social mission* of these institutions that matters most – what they publicly stand for. Not the number of bureaucrats or rules they enlist. In other words, approaching the question of bureaucracy from only a quantitative perspective misses the point. We need to see this as a *qualitative* issue. Some big bureaucracies can be brilliant for society, a beacon of progress. Whereas some very small ones can be horrible – anti-social, even.

When we approach bureaucracy from this qualitative angle, it's easy to see why so many have failed over the last thirty years. For example, a cash-starved state agency that's been ordered to act like a private business – as austerity-led politicians insist – will surely deliver a bad service. How could it not? Similarly, it shouldn't surprise us if a large corporation that's cornered the market in a monopolistic fashion comes to hate its customers. The ones who complain are a particular inconvenience.

For simplicity's sake, we might call these *bad bureaucracies*.

An apt example is the UK Home Office, which processes immigration and visa applications. This has recently become a truly awful institution.

A 2017 report found that the Home Office makes an astounding 800 per cent profit on immigration applications, often involving families who are eligible to reside in the UK but are forced to jump through innumerable hoops.[61] Many applications are rejected on a technicality. When this happens, the applicant is free to apply again . . . but also pay again (an unfathomable £2,297 per person for an Indefinite Leave to Remain visa). Customer services – if that is what we must call them – have been subcontracted to a private company called Sitel UK. Some immediate changes ensued, of course. Anyone wanting to email the Home Office about a visa application is charged £5.48.[62] Not only does the Home Office function like a horrible corporation (or 'racket', some might say), it turns out that their staff aren't treated much better. The institution has suffered budget cuts of 24.9 per cent during recent years.[63] The UK Border Force – a flagship division of the Home Office – conducted an internal survey of staff morale and discovered that less than 1 in 4 workers were satisfied with senior management.[64] An insider said that workers 'see their senior managers as having no leadership skills and no idea what they are doing at all. They fear for the future of the work they do and their own jobs with waves of cuts. Morale has never been lower and yet it amazingly continues to plummet.' This bureaucracy has *very bad* written all over it.

I'm interested in good bureaucracies instead, ones that deliver pooled public goods in the name of progress and dignity . . . people's bureaucracies.

In *The Road to Serfdom*, Hayek argued that no such organizations could ever exist. We're all too different and our values vary so much across society. He concludes that, because we cannot agree on what is 'good', everyone should simply follow their own path instead, guided by self-interest and the price mechanism. Well, try telling that to the families who lost loved ones in the Grenfell Tower disaster. Or the victim of food contamination writhing in pain. There isn't much variance in values there! Hayek is wrong: there are community goods that most of us recognize, especially when they are violated. A socially purposeful or 'good' bureaucracy seeks to enable and facilitate these social goods in an empowering and democratic manner.

Some thinkers make a useful distinction between bureaucracies that are coercive and those more enabling.[65] Coercive bureaucracies treat their own members and clients as objects. They are there to be processed. We have seen plenty of coercive bureaucracies in recent years, with the neoliberalization of the state and its corporate partnerships. They especially mushroom in authoritarian and totalitarian settings, which have become an important characteristic of capitalism recently.[66] It is important to note that such organizations are hardly ever bureaucratized at the top, since the organizational apex is cushioned by administrative secrecy and privilege.[67] The elites ardently impose discipline on their workforce and public, but seldom apply the same rigour to themselves (for example, look at how senior bureaucrats award themselves massive pay rises but suddenly become miserly penny-pinchers when it comes to their workforce).

Enabling bureaucracies, on the other hand, are designed to empower people, particularly in relation to democratic involvement and social betterment. For example, one simply could not organize an amazing public healthcare system like the National Health Service without an element of enabling formalism. What's more, this type of bureaucracy is great for achieving a degree of procedural and distributive justice related to workers' rights, gender equality and discrimination (which shouldn't be conflated with kadi (or sharia) justice or personal stewardship). Because of this 'levelling' quality, Max Weber was ambivalent about bureaucracy. Sure, it might dehumanize the world and render it rather machinic. On the other side of the coin, however, 'bureaucracy inevitably accompanies modern mass democracy'.[68] This arises from

the demand for equality before the law in the personal and functional sense – hence the horror of 'privilege', and the principled rejection of doing business 'from case to case'. The non-bureaucratic administration of any large social structure rests in some way upon the fact that existing social, material or honorific preferences and ranks are connected with administrative functions and duties.[69]

Weber calls this the 'great levelling' of social differences that frequently accompanies administrative bureaucracy. Strangely, this feature gives organized formalism something of an *emancipatory* flavour when it comes into contact with the underprivileged and exploited.

Radical Bureaucracies

Weber wasn't naïve, of course. He understood how the bureaucratic form can easily turn into an oligarchical regime, despite its levelling influences elsewhere. But it can also serve to *politicize* its members and wider community, unsettling important power relationships associated with capitalism. Labour economist Richard Edwards noted this, back in the late 1970s.[70] *Contested Terrain*, his classic study of battles between labour and big business in the USA, is still worth reading today. During the course of industrialization in America, Edwards identifies three successive phases of control used by bosses to manage workers.

The first was simple control or direct observation. Arbitrary acts of authority were rife, of course. When workers finally unionized to counteract the personal tyranny of supervisors, technology had caught up. Thus, simple control was replaced by a second system: technical control or the assembly line. This kept order for a while, but strikes and sabotage were soon commonplace. So employers deployed a third mode of control with the help of bureaucracy. This entailed rules and regulations, but also career paths and due process in relation to grievances. According to Edwards, bureaucracy ironically proved to be a double-edged sword for corporations. On the one hand, it oppressed workers with machine-like precision. But, on the other, it unwittingly gave employees access to a new vocabulary of rights and responsibilities, exposing their otherwise isolated workplaces to wider struggles unfolding at the national level. Edwards explains with characteristic brilliance:

> Bureaucratic control thus established an explicit structure around which broader struggles in the political arena coalesce. These struggles provide an immediate avenue for improving the contradictions of wage labor, and they may have more revolutionary consequences by linking workplace struggle with class conflict in society at large. For bureaucratic control is merely the latest form in which capitalist development socializes the process of production; by constructing formal rights and responsibilities, capitalists have abolished the individual capitalist's responsibility for working conditions and replaced it with a social accountability. Thus does modern control resolve the problem of local conflict only at the cost of raising it to a more general level.[71]

The trend that Edwards describes here was abruptly halted with the election of Ronald Reagan in 1981, and the neoliberal war on bureaucracy. Workers were constituted as self-styled human capitalists soon after and, with subsequent waves of computerization, the conditions were being ripened for wiki-feudalism. Something similar happened in the UK with the election of Margaret Thatcher and her infatuation with F. A. Hayek. It cleared a path for an economic paradigm that would later be characterized by zero-hours contracts and Uberized ghost jobs. In this regard, it seems incredible today that employers once used long-term career paths to control workers, even in menial jobs. It's a rare thing to see now, which tells us how far things have shifted to the political right.

In light of Edwards' fascinating analysis, we can see why the neoliberal power elite hate bureaucracy so much. For a period in the 1960s and 1970s, the legal codification of jobs in the USA and UK teetered on the edge of a *radical democratization* of work. The labour movement was becoming wildly federated. Ordinary people acquired rights and smartened up under this system, no longer befuddled or fearful, but a threat to the class hierarchy. Now all the pieces of the puzzle fall into place. Hayek and his followers were not against planning *per se*, but *counter-planning*, the bread-and-butter activities of the workers' movement.[72] The prattle about being yourself, individual choice and difference/diversity that has dominated the ideology of work since the 1990s makes complete sense in this respect. It helped break unions and water down democratic involvement, and was a handy excuse for financial capitalists to withdraw from the Keynesian social compact.

Steve Hilton's criticism of bureaucracy wants to look like a grassroots fight against the establishment. But it isn't. He is instead extending one of its leading themes, Hayekian individualism, albeit camouflaged in 'peace' T-shirts and sentimental humanism. Happy, shiny people populate Hilton's world, for they've been liberated from the clutches of mindless red tape. Digital technology widens these freedoms in undulating waves of e-positivity. But this isn't what we witnessed the night of the Grenfell Tower blaze. No apps were available to save these victims. The bonfire of the building regulations licked at their doors and the cries for help went unanswered. And the terrible inferno that ensued? Definitely a symptom of a society in major decline.

Chapter Four

The Human . . .
All-Too-Human Workplace

In 2015, the Las Vegas-based online shoe and clothing store Zappos was regularly in the news. To convey what type of culture the firm had, almost every article had a prominent image of an employee in casual dress, relaxing in office space overflowing with personal items. Batman figures. Beach balls. Collages. Surfboards. Teddy bears. Empty Coke cans. Handcrafted posters reading 'Whose Yo Daddy?' and 'No Boys Allowed'.

In contrast to the lifeless office settings we usually associate with big companies, it was clear that Zappos was doing things differently. The enterprise had grown rapidly, with annual sales of more than US$1 billion in the last few years. Then, in 2014, Zappos CEO Tony Hsieh read a book called *Reinventing Organizations* by management consultant Frederic Laloux.[1] It completely changed the way Hsieh saw the business.[2]

Laloux argued that self-organization and flat structures are far superior to the conventional, vertical bureaucracies that have dominated industrial capitalism. Horizontal organizations use self-management rather than a top-down chain of command. That makes them more responsive, agile and empowering to workers because they regulate their own tasks and responsibilities. For Laloux this represents an evolutionary leap forward in how jobs are organized. The reinvented organization is 'not the pyramid we know. There are no job descriptions, no targets, hardly any budgets. In their place come many new and soulful practices that make for extraordinarily productive and purposeful organizations.'[3] Despite these findings, big bureaucracies continue to be the norm, unfortunately, an obstacle to achieving a higher, more human form of social consciousness.

The reason *Reinventing Organizations* resonated with Hsieh is because he was restructuring Zappos.[4] He'd recently informed the company's 1,500 employees – or Zapponians – that the firm was adopting a system called 'Holacracy' (a term derived from Greek: ὅλον, *holon* or 'whole').[5] Instead of traditional management hierarchies, Zappos would be made up of circles. These independent units would manage their own workflow, whilst remaining reliant on the organization as a whole (hence the term 'Holacracy'). There'd be no more bosses, job titles or any of the other red tape connected with bureaucracy. Holacracy is about enabling people to manage themselves, trusting them as capable adults who thrive on flexibility and creativity. In place of static job titles, for example, workers will use a system called 'badging', which is more fluid and adaptable to new challenges. After Hsieh's announcement, workers had to prove their expertise in order to continue in their current roles. This applied to new recruits and veteran Zapponians alike.[6]

So far, this might look like a weird experiment in anarcho-socialism. But far from it. For Hsieh, the management approach was quintessentially entrepreneurial, taking its inspiration from capitalist individualism and the wonders of private enterprise. If anything, this was an experiment in *100 per cent pure capitalism*. In an interview, Hsieh compared Zappos to the real-time supply-and-demand method pioneered by Uber: 'An Uber driver doesn't have a shift. They can decide to show up or not show up . . . we want to apply that same thing to incoming phone calls. Holacracy, open market, badging – all are going to be a huge part of it.'[7]

A deep informal culture obviously had to complement this unstructured way of organizing the labour process, otherwise nothing would get done.[8] Zappos prided itself in this regard. Employees were not obliged to erase their personal lives before starting work each morning. Zapponians could be themselves in the office – hence the images mentioned earlier of employees decorating their cubicles with personal items and fun slogans. According to Laloux, workers who are free to 'be themselves' are ultimately happier and more productive. One curious journalist sat in on a staff meeting to see what it was like being a Zapponian. The meeting 'began with "checkins and checkouts," in which each participant (including me) was expected to speak about how they were feeling – about their work, their personal struggles'.[9] Unlike previous attempts to build cultures of commitment in US corporations – where workers are rewarded for outward conformity – Zapponians didn't have to fake it. All feelings are welcome. A Zappos manager explains: 'when you have a culture that values so much of people's quirkiness and emotional state and outwardly being kind, cheerful, generous, and happy, sometimes you can make it seem like it's not OK – even in a very subtle way – to not be happy all the time'.[10] This organization, however, imposed no such emotional limitations and celebrated authentic views and values.

E for Exodus

But soon there was a problem. The new company structure (or lack thereof) was not to everyone's liking and discontent spread through the workforce.[11] It appeared the concept of Holacracy was difficult to understand: complex and opaque. After other gripes became prevalent in early 2015, Hsieh sent a long memo to staff. They were warned it would take at least 30 minutes to read. Following Laloux's lead, a major new philosophical principle was being added to Zappos, called 'Teal':

> Teal organizations attempt to minimize service provider groups and lean more towards creating self-organizing and self-managing business-centric groups instead. As of 4/30/15, in order to eliminate the legacy of management hierarchy, there will effectively be no more people managers.[12]

Hsieh also recommended all Zapponians read *Reinventing Organizations*. Then he took a gamble . . . known as 'the offer'. Zappos had been using this idea in its recruitment process for some time.[13] Upon completing their training, new recruits would be offered a payment of $2,000 *not* to take the job and to leave. Human Resources believed that this would sort out the wheat from the chaff, with only genuine Zapponians choosing to stay. Now, given all the discontent, Hsieh applied the principle to all employees, in the hope of flushing out the troublemakers. If they don't like the new boss-less culture, then Zappos will pay them three months' salary to go elsewhere.[14] Staff started to leave in droves. Of the 1,500, 18 per cent took buy-outs, and another 11 per cent simply left without a package.[15] By 2016, it was reported that the turnover rate had reached 30 per cent.[16]

Back in 2014, Hsieh's plans to rid Zappos of formal job titles and structures was widely celebrated in the business press. But the knives came out when Holacracy crashed and burned in 2016. Ex-Zapponians were asked about their decision to leave. One said Holacracy is 'a social experiment [that] created chaos and uncertainty'.[17] Even employees who remained with the company raised doubts about it. For example, payroll inevitably requires a systematic and even bureaucratic approach in order to function correctly. But that contradicted the ethos of Holacracy. As one manager said in relation to pay grades, 'right now we're trying to figure out what is that world going to look like, and how do we fairly compensate people in that system?'[18] Another employee complained, 'at Zappos there's so much implicit stuff you're supposed to do because it's part of the culture'.[19] One Zapponian recalled a meeting she attended where Hsieh discussed the negative feedback. She was disappointed: 'I would have liked to hear some actions that may be taken to address how drastically approval of managers and legacy leadership has fallen, and how strongly more and more employees are feeling like favouritism is becoming a bigger problem.'[20]

The Nightmare of Participation

The attempt to deformalize big organizations *à la* Zappos has been a prominent feature of corporate management ideology since the 1990s. Californian notions like 'liberation management' and the importance of economic self-sufficiency, personal relationships and 'adhocracy' (making things up as you go) are meant to inspire a more human-friendly workplace.[21] To do this, CEOs needed to take a very different approach to organizing jobs. Since the dawn of industrialism capitalism, owners had been at war with employees, literally stripping them of their humanity in the name of efficiency and profit. That's why employees would avoid these environments like the plague if they had the choice. Who could blame them? A life trapped in grey, boring bureaucracies isn't appealing to anyone. As with the factory, they operate on the assumption that workers leave everything unique and special about themselves at home before clocking in. Bland uniformity and simmering resentment tend to characterize such cultures.

The 'Californian turn' in managerial thought ostensibly sought to reconnect individuals with their jobs – not through socially orientated methods, but by applying strict capitalist individualism to the office.[22] And this is where things get interesting because such individualism was packaged in rather left-wing language, often Marxian-inspired themes, particularly the call to abandon devitalizing bureaucracies and allow workers to organize themselves.[23] Now it was the corporate elite, not only trade unions, that was speaking of the death of management. Employees should manage themselves, like mini-enterprises. Following this intellectual seizure and repackaging of radical humanism (deploying phrases we might have seen on the streets of Paris during the May '68 uprising), market individualism had found the perfect narrative for redefining jobs, all in the name of making corporations more people-friendly.[24]

It is important to note that, despite all the fanfare about liberation management – from the 1990s up to the arrival of Holacracy – most firms continued to hire managers to watch over workers, use bureaucratic hierarchies, and so forth.[25] Moreover, for all the talk about worker empowerment, none of the tenets of capitalism were challenged by this shift, with the precepts of private property and commodified labour even deepened in the process. Nevertheless, the change in ideological tone represents a sort of weathervane concerning how neoliberal capitalism wants us to see it in the present context. The subliminal message is something like this: until now you've always believed that your authentic self was symbolically outside the moment of paid labour. Now Holacracy and liberation management, however, invite you to entertain a degree of overlap. You can now enter the neoliberal enterprise and retain a modicum of humanity, after all. On the surface, it appears as if corporate managerialism is finally compromising and bending to the needs of individual workers, more appreciative of the real you. But in fact the Californian turn is about hastening the opposite: an individual fully absorbed by capitalism.

When the Zappos exodus caught the attention of the media, some thought it illustrated a cold fact that critics of capitalism never want to hear. Employees actually like hierarchies.[26] Anecdotal research had been available for some time in this regard.[27] It turns out that workers find authority structures psychologically comforting – the more, the better. Workers are attracted to the bureaucracies that Zappos got rid of because the 'pecking order' helps them plan career progression. Yearning for a boss might even be part our DNA, a product of evolutionary design, according to Stanford University researchers: 'it may come from the drive to have one's genetic material survive, which requires being able to first discern and then associate oneself with the individuals and groups most likely to win in fights for survival'.[28] Clinical psychologist and controversial darling of the right Jordan Peterson even suggests that humans aren't all that different from lobsters, which are innately attuned (via serotonin runs) to status/hierarchy.[29] Thus, questioning hierarchy (or in his words, 'Western patriarchy') is tantamount to challenging millions of years of evolutionary history.

With proclamations like these circulating widely, it's easy to see why some might interpret the problems at Zappos in the same light. But I don't think Zappos employees left because they had a burning desire to be dominated or even needed the cash. Indeed, perhaps the opposite. Does anyone really want to work in a climate where your livelihood is completely reliant on the unpredictable and subjective judgements of others – in other words, whether your team (or 'circle') leader likes you today (and yes, Zappos still had bosses, of course, including the CEO, which everybody understood despite Tony Hsieh's pretending he was just one of the team)? In terms of basic employment issues like pay, workload, promotion and disciplinary procedures, the last thing any worker desires is for it to be arbitrary. Echoing the concerns of the Zappos employee above, it's not hard to see why favouritism and pettiness might flourish in organizations that embrace Holacracy. Of course, impersonal rules, procedures and protocols can also be used against workers, which in times of economic recession has become the forte of most HR departments today. But, by the same token, an element of objective due process is still probably preferable compared to a situation in which your line-manager wants to be your friend before considering a promotion, or being kept awake at night by the mind games of an office bully.[30]

Networking with Evil

It's strange that the quest to make work more people-friendly is framed by most pro-business gurus as a question of economic deregulation, rendering jobs discretionary and subjective. What exactly is more human about that? Take the annual performance appraisal, for instance. In many organizations, this is closely tied to promotion and remuneration. According to Steve Hilton in his book *More Human*, discussed earlier concerning his war on big bureaucracy, these appraisals shouldn't be weighed down by red tape – too cold and impersonal. Instead, 'the more human alternative is also the one that, more simply, improves performance: frequent, informal meetings'.[31] Of course, what's suspiciously omitted here is the important fact that appraisal meetings are often the only official forum where workers can air grievances and have them acted upon. Sure, in the current climate they can be used by intrusive middle-managers to turn up the heat. But they can ironically also provide *social protection* for employees, especially when a militant union rep also gets involved.

Like Hilton, Tony Hsieh, too, trades in the cult of informality, arguing for more personal employment relationships. He once imparted some advice to aspiring corporate networkers in Ivanka Trump's business book *Trump Card*.[32] Hsieh's method was carefully gleaned from his own experiences as a professional networker. Being yourself is central:

> My advice is to stop trying to 'network' in the traditional business sense, and instead just try to build up the number and depth of your friendships, where the friendship itself is its own reward. The more diverse your set of friendships are, the more likely you'll derive both personal and business benefits from your friendship later down the road. You won't know exactly what those benefits will be, but if your friendships are genuine, those benefits will magically appear 2–3 years later down the road.[33]

This sounds horribly instrumental, to be sure – but also oblivious to the role that official distance plays when it comes to making social life endurable in contexts riven with strong power relationships (i.e., late capitalism). As any seasoned worker in the post-industrial world knows only too well, as soon as the boss asks to get personal, or even worse, then you're in big trouble. It's not as if you can decline the offer. And, if you agree, it might turn out fine . . . but also it might not. In this sense, any organization that seeks to cultivate a more human environment requires the *extra-individual* protocols of legal formalism in case things gets nasty. A sense of procedural and distributive equality is crucial. Otherwise, organizational life can easily descend into some kind of brutal hell-hole.

Take what happened in the Australian branch of marketing giant

Appco. It was recently labelled the most humiliating workplace in Australia.[34] First, there was the use of bogus contracting, with employees hired as independent business owners and subsequently paid below the minimum wage. This triggered an investigation that revealed incredible levels of harassment. Workers spoke of degrading stunts and rituals imposed by management when sales targets weren't met. For example, leaked videos show underperformers competing in the 'slug race', where they writhe around on the office floor with arms behind their backs. Another captures employees being forced to become chickens and have a cockfight. As an Appco worker explains, 'it was every Friday morning. The idea is, like being a bird, you wrestle each other to the ground, and you have to try and hold them down for three seconds.'[35]

Other exercises were revealed: 'As it turned out, the punishment for not hitting their target was to shove a cigarette up your bottom, pull it out and then smoke it.'[36] Workers are in the process of taking an AU$85 million class action against Appco Australia, accusing the firm of 'sham contracting'. When asked about the case, a lawyer describes yet another clip he viewed, pointing out that the stunt was actually orchestrated by the senior managers:

> The video depicts a series of pseudo-sexual acts performed on men by other men . . . It's a video that can't be explained in any employment or any business context . . . It appears to be the relic of a very long lost navy ritual that we don't see in the Australian context anymore.[37]

Clearly something was very wrong at Appco Australia. This organization is melding both cold market individualism – employees had been classified as independent contractors – and the demented informalism of an 'all-too-human' power relationship. It was the Marquis de Sade who first demonstrated how the unimaginable terrors that human cruelty can inspire don't necessarily contradict the calculative sobriety of reason – particularly economic reason.[38] Measuring, counting and contractualization can easily coexist with, and even complement, egregious malice. Appco Australia helps us see why. Structural economic insecurity and rationalization (or what neoliberal economists call an unregulated labour market) seamlessly interconnect with the devolved fickleness of personal relations so enthusiastically advocated by Californian management thinkers.

Death of a Professor

It must be remembered that the localism being encouraged here is not of the socialist, familial or communal kind, although it appears to tap into a certain form of *tradition*, as the lawyer indicated above. No, this is all about economic libertarianism, a monetary transaction in which almost anything goes. This actually requires a *great deal of sociality* to function . . . mostly of the negative kind, in the form of administrative shock tactics, mind games and intimidation, lurking in the shadows of economic rationality. When expressed in this nominally objective and 'data driven' environment, bullying isn't a deviation from numerical reason but a subtle extension of it. The cash value of the individual is calculated by their willingness to go along with the subjective whims of arbitrary power-holders. Thus, an unorthodox interpenetration takes place. The informal/subjective domain becomes a crucible for establishing one's cost-effectiveness in a purely quantitative sense.

This curious blend of impersonal economic prudence and excessive cruelty doesn't just occur in private businesses, of course. One of the worst offenders at the moment is the University. This is particularly so with the rise of the 'all-administrative university' and its open assault on teaching faculty and researchers, who have largely been cowered into silence.[39] The tragic death in 2014 of Stefan Grimm, a professor of toxicology at Imperial College London, illustrates the perils faced in the all-administrative university, where a growing cadre of technocrats treat the institution as a profit centre and its workforce as disposable contractors. Professor Grimm was found dead at his home, having committed suicide.

One month after his death, everyone in Grimm's department received an email from the dead academic, apparently written prior to his suicide and sent via a delayed timer. The subject heading read 'How Professors are treated at Imperial College' and claimed 'this is not a university anymore but a business'.[40] Grimm was under immense pressure to secure more research grants, an important performance metric for staff and the government's Research Assessment Exercise.[41] Was he being singled out personally? In his ghostly email, Grimm describes an encounter with the head of department:

> On May 30th '13 my boss came into my office together with his PA and asked me what grants I had. After I enumerated them I was told that this was not enough and that I had to leave the College within one year – 'max' as he said . . . Without any further comment he left my office. It was only then that I realized that he did not even have the courtesy to close the door of my office when he delivered this message. When I turned around the corner I saw a student who seems to have overheard the conversation looking at me in utter horror.[42]

After this distressing meeting, Grimm received an email that read: 'please be aware that this constitutes the start of informal action in relation to your performance'. Grimm's death has been widely attributed to workplace bullying and stress (the coroner called his demise 'needless').[43] However, according to the evidence we have, the harassment he experienced was not of the impulsive kind – a boss momentarily losing his head or a bully operating outside the parameters of officialdom. No, his treatment was integral to the official system (e.g., how many research grants have you successfully obtained?), but could only be properly activated via an act of deformalization, the in-your-face 'informal review process' mentioned above, whereby Grimm's targets are personally overseen by his supervisor.[44] Cold metrics and hot intimidation are but different sides of the same coin.[45] The blend signals a significant shift in the way technocracy is enacted. For example, just look at the awful email Grimm was sent by his head of department:

> I am of the opinion that you are struggling to fulfil the metrics of a Professorial post at Imperial College . . .You have previously initiated discussions in our meetings regarding opportunities outside of Imperial College and I know you have been exploring opportunities elsewhere. Should this be the direction you wish to pursue, then I will do what I can to help you succeed.[46]

What sort of ideology can spawn such a troubling amalgam of heartless individualism, ultra-objective metrics and close-contact trauma? In my opinion, Grimm's death has neoclassical economics written all over it, especially that of F. A. Hayek and his quest to radically decollectivize the workforce. From this perspective, labour is (theoretically, at least) outside the firm that they technically work for, and thus *secondary* as a rule, no matter how much that organization relies upon their efforts. Few were surprised by the response of Alice Gast – Rector of Imperial College – to the death of Professor Grimm, in a radio interview. Today, according to her, university professors are 'really like small business owners . . . they have their own research and they have their research funding to look after . . . It's a very highly competitive world out there.'[47]

iCapitalism

It's the perverse individualization of jobs at Appco and Imperial College that stands out. Workers are treated as external and independent enterprises that are meant to compete in an open and challenging environment. This is a central principle of Uberization and its fixation on the *de-organization* of work (for labour at least, not the multinational corporation or the plutocracy, who use organizations very effectively indeed). As discussed in an earlier chapter, the idea has been a staple part of neoclassical economics since the 1980s. The semantics shift from organizations to networks and then to self-regulating individuals. Organizational economist Herbert Simon even joked that the very idea of a workforce was being replaced by 'independent windowless Leibnizian monads'.[48]

The recent popularity of on-demand work systems, including zero-hours contracts, self-employment and freelancing, is indicative of this trend. From an employer's perspective, the economic rationale is obvious. It allows the business to push many of the costs of employment back on to the employee and the state, in terms of tax credits and accommodation benefits. If capitalism is built on the tenet of socializing its endogenous costs and contradictions, then Uberization is an acute expression of this. Take the traditional role of supervision, for example. Why incur the expense of hiring managers when the task of surveillance and control can be passed on to the customer instead, via the rating systems used by Lyft and Airtasker?

There are additional benefits to employers. While the expense of hiring a worker is dramatically reduced in this arrangement, *labour output* is steadily increased, mainly because jobs are no longer enclosed by fixed hours. So-called 'flexible employment systems' significantly lengthen the working day because individuals are potentially *always on call*, while still only being paid for the specific work they do. Employers can thus have their cake and eat it too. A major study of European workplaces found that the more flexible (and thus uncertain) a job is, the more unpaid overtime workers find themselves doing.[49]

Having labour carry a significantly increased proportion of the costs (typically on their credit cards) is a more efficient way for employers to increase output, compared to labour intensification within a set number of hours, because the latter requires investment in technology and supervisory commitment. Of course, economic efficiency is in the eye of the beholder. While this all looks great to the employer, it's often very *inefficient* and expensive for everyone else.

City Sewer

With all the apps and high-tech paraphernalia involved, the Uberization of jobs has futuristic and 'brave new world' connotations in the public imagination. But the underlying principle is not really that new. In some respects, the attempt to make workers individually responsible for systemic-level deficiencies has been around since the inception of industrial capitalism, something Karl Marx was attentive to. In the sixth chapter of *Capital*, Marx observes that for capitalism to function at all – as the exploitation of labour – it must ensure that the worker is *formally free* as the sole owner of his or labour power.[50] It might seem like a strange thing to say, given how Marx was writing about men, women and children enslaved in dangerous and dirty factory conditions. And who would ever call workers at Appco, or Stefan Grimm, free?

But Marx had an important point. Only when workers are legally free to sell their labour time (to this or that employer, or not at all) can the capitalist effectively use them to make a profit. There can be no *official servitude* here, because that would mean the worker 'converting himself from a free man into a slave, from an owner of a commodity into a commodity'.[51] Why does it make any difference? Marx pursues the line of thought:

> In order that its possessor [of labour power] may sell it as a commodity, he must have it at his disposal, he must be the free proprietor of his own labour capacity, hence of his person. He and the owner of money meet in the market, and enter into relations with each other on a foot of equality as owners of commodities, with the sole difference that one is a buyer, the other a seller; both are therefore equal in the eyes of the law.[52]

This is purely theoretical freedom, of course. In reality, workers clearly do end up helplessly dependent on an employer, mere wage-slaves with little choice about the matter. Marx is trying to demonstrate the ideological preconditions that capitalism requires for this *de facto* servitude to function: how the system must portray itself to ensure the concrete subordination of workers. Let's turn the argument around. If the worker was *legally owned* by his or her employer (i.e., slavery), then the business would be entirely responsible for his/her upkeep and so forth. As Marx shows, peonage is very expensive for the master to maintain and time-consuming from a business perspective. Formally free workers on the other hand are accountable for their own existence – hence, Marx's great insight. On the surface, this appears to be a paradigm shift towards increased personal liberty – and it is, in some respects. But this is a highly delimited freedom, whose enactment (e.g., I chose this job, rather than that) obfuscates the wider structural unfreedoms that define our existence in the economy (e.g., unlike a slave, I'm free to leave my job, but also free to live under a bridge if I can't find work). This kind of perverted freedom acts as a salve to help smooth a path to the workhouse, something it continues to do to this day.

For example, take the super-reliance our economy still has on fossil fuels today, and the coming Anthropocene, which might soon see global capitalism committing mass ecocide. In his excellent book *Fossil Capital*, Andreas Malm reveals how this dependence on steam-power and coal was not inevitable.[53] In early industrial England, *waterpower* was in fact considered superior to steam. Water was free and renewable. Factory owners didn't have to pay for the extraction of coal. And, as a result, watermills inevitably sprang up across the country. There was only one catch, however. Watermills were constrained by location: mainly rivers in unpopulated areas. Therefore, industrialists had to attract workers and build special colonies to house them. These colonies began to adopt qualities we would associate with the slave plantation, which made the venture incredibly expensive: 'the appropriation of waterpower generally necessitated a process of ingathering of labour power, of concentrating workers from all possible directions on the spot . . . at first, the mill-owners may have subsisted on local reserves, but as their businesses expanded they would have to scrape together operatives from a widening catchment area and billet them in lodgings paid for from their own pockets'.[54]

In effect, owners were forced to construct and maintain entire villages. Coal power and steam engines, on the other hand, were *mobile* and could be placed near and around cities. Upon receiving a wage, 'free workers' took care of themselves and absorbed the social injuries of class by carrying them out of the factory gates when the shift ended. Cities grew for this reason, and this is a key reason they thrived despite their unmanageability. On this count, perhaps it's no coincidence that Zappos CEO Tony Hsieh mentioned the city when celebrating the Uber-model: 'we want Zappos to function more like a city and less like a top-down bureaucratic organization'.[55] Artists like Lou Reed saw things in their true light, however: not the cosmopolitan paradise Zappos had in mind, but something closer to a circus or sewer.

Market individualism has nothing to do with proper free choice, of course, because real freedom involves the ability to step back and not decide (the power of voluntary exit from the decision-making matrix presented to us), whereas here we're speaking more about a *false choice*. The worker has no option other than to sell their labour power / time to an employer, but *technically* it's still the worker's choice as to whether this happens or not. Hence the obsession with individual freedom so endlessly touted by neoclassical economists and Californian management gurus alike. The idea is clearly underpinned by a paradox. Sure, I don't have to work for KFC and tolerate my abusive supervisor. But when I look out of the window and see a homeless person begging in the rain, I realize how highly constrained that choice actually is. I'm only truly free to be unfree ... and equally unfree in my very *capacity* to choose. This thin veil of formalism ironically plants a high degree of informal discretion at the centre of my job. What my Hitlerite boss thinks of me – my personality, attitudes, likes and dislikes – now suddenly becomes painfully relevant to my predicament, since only that stands between me and the beggar in the rain. In the end, I get on with frying chicken.

App-fascism

Uberization certainly looks high-tech and flashy, the product of a brave new age. But some researchers argue we should reject the futuristic gloss surrounding the gig economy.[56] While the technology is undoubtedly impressive, Uber-jobs are more properly situated in business systems prevalent during the early industrial period. To see why, we have to differentiate regular jobs from those that are now shaped by digital platforms. Four features of the 'gig economy' stand out in this regard. Jobs may consist of: (1) on-call work (labour is employed and paid only when needed, with no guaranteed hours); (2) piece-work compensation (workers are paid according to a specific job or task, not by the hour or the day); (3) provision of own equipment (employees supply the capital needed, such as a car); and (4) nominal status of independence (workers are reclassified as independent contractors, which means statutory requirements like paid sick leave and employer pension contributions don't apply).

These features strongly resemble the 'putting out' system widely used in the early nineteenth century. A merchant capitalist gave employees raw materials and they worked on them at home using their own equipment. Work hours were largely unfixed and irregular, determined by surges in demand. Labour was accordingly compensated on a piece-rate basis. And self-employment and independent contracting was widespread before the arrival of regular jobs in the twentieth century. If we subtract the technology, then employment practices commonplace 200 years ago are perhaps the real inspiration behind the gig economy and Uberization today. As employment researcher Jim Stanford puts it, 'apart from the specific nature of digital methods of communication, work allocation, supervision and payment, the work practices and relationships embodied in modern digital platform businesses do not seem "new" at all'.[57]

If they were so beneficial to the employer, then why were these old Uber-techniques phased out in the twentieth century (only to make a surprising reappearance in the app-saturated twenty-first century)? Standardized technology and skill growth were important, but the decisive factor was a recalcitrant labour movement that demanded fairer treatment from employers.[58] The casualized nature of these jobs allowed abusive gangmasters to establish autarchic fiefdoms over their workforce. Life under a gangmaster was unpredictable and highly interpersonal, which made it particularly terrifying.[59] Victims found themselves mere playthings of sadistic bosses, with few protections from the state. Labour unions fought back, and their growing demand for social justice was ratified by governments building up to and following World War II, only to be reversed in the 1980s when 'risk' and 'insecurity' became cultural virtues, and having a job a privilege. We can see why the gangmaster mentality might be making a comeback in the context of neoliberalism and the decline of regular jobs[60] – only this time with an added technological twist, exposing more and more workers to what we might call *app-fascism*.

App-fascism is rife in the modern workplace. Take Amazon's recent patenting of a vibrating wristband to direct its warehouse workers or 'associates'. The device will not only track where workers are in the building at all times, but vibrate to nudge them in the correct (and most efficient) direction.[61] The term 'nudge' originates from behaviour economics, a creepy sub-discipline that blends psychological manipulation into its models. Uber have applied its insights (such as 'loss aversion') to keep drivers on the road longer and control them more effectively.[62] US recruitment firm Crossover has plumbed new depths in relation to electronic surveillance. In order to keep tabs on its remote freelancers, a system called WorkSmart is used.[63] Webcam photographs are taken every 10 minutes to check whether workers are at their computers, and this data is linked to keystroke rates and app use. A 'focus score' and 'intensity score' are then created to evaluate their performance. When an industry specialist was asked about this level of surveillance, he said: 'If you are a parent and you have a teenage son or daughter coming home late and not doing their homework, you might wonder what they are doing. It's the same as employees.'[64]

Digital Endarkenment

We could be forgiven for thinking that nothing could be more contemporary and 'forward thinking' than the modern fitness centre. Yet a recent study found, however, an environment in which personal trainers are entrapped in work arrangements that couldn't really be termed 'modern'.[65] Trainers are self-employed and hired on a just-in-time, supply-and-demand basis. But that's only the start. They also have to pay to access the fitness centre. And because they're considered independent contractors, the financial overheads are largely shouldered by them alone. However, this icy economic rationality is accompanied by an expectation of patrimonial deference – acquiring future clients depends upon personal connections with managers and existing clients. Technically, this is something we should only find in pre-capitalist economies. So researchers termed this employment situation *neo-villeiny* because it 'reflects the defining characteristics of a villein, a work relationship that existed in medieval Britain between serfs and lords. These characteristics are: bondage to the landlord/employer; payment of rent to the landlord/employer; no guarantee of any income (rent merely guarantees the opportunity to earn); and extensive unpaid and speculative work that is highly beneficial to the landlord/employer.'[66]

The summation fits with the experiences of trainers. Some said they felt bonded to a specific gym because that was their only source of income. There was little mobility between gyms because of the opportunity costs. Moreover, payment could be erratic and unpredictable, a feature shared with other platform business models. As a result, trainers had to form special relationships with employers in order to work the best hours. After establishing the terms and conditions of bondage, instructors rented time at fitness centres to conduct their work and network with potential clients. This rent cost between £350 and £450 per calendar month, but could be reduced if trainers helped out with staffing, cleaned the toilets and gave extra classes. Such 'payment-in-kind' arrangements were, of course, a central feature of medieval serfdom and 'prebendal' economic relationships.[67]

The study found other fascinating aspects in this line of work, particularly *unpaid speculative labour*. For example, a personal trainer called Alfie said: 'you have to be out there with clients, booking taster sessions and getting known'. He worked a 60-hour week with at least half of that 'talking to people, getting to know them. That's what gets you business.'[68] Work inevitably gets very personal. Trainers had to keep the gym bosses happy, of course, but also clients. One trainer said, 'you need to talk to people, to get to know them. You have to show an interest in them. The personality is very important. They always say that people don't buy the product, they buy the person.'[69]

The Road to Serfdom, the title of Hayek's famous homage to capitalist individualism certainly takes on new meaning in light of this study. When it comes to pay and conditions, work like this represents a major step backwards, literally into the Dark Ages.

'Full-Fat' Society

We're often told by the critics of austerity-led capitalism that it's painfully dehumanizing to most of us. All relationships are reduced to naked self-interest and this has devastated the very fabric of society in England and the USA, where the only thing people know for sure is that they're on their own. However, as the cases above illustrate, deregulation and the burning of red tape (all in the name of being 'more human', of course) has made capitalism almost *too personal*.

This widening sphere of negative or inverse informality is often missed by critics of neoliberalism. For example, Wolfgang Streeck argues, in *How Will Capitalism End?*, that years of austerity have created post-social societies in Europe, or what he dubs 'society lite'.[70] Government regimes that support strict fiscal discipline and budget cuts have basically helped to eviscerate entire communities, transforming society into a kind of Lippmannian spectacle or demented cinema, where isolated individuals passively look on as humanity is hollowed out.

The bleak diagnosis certainly rings true. But let's look at fiscal austerity from a different angle. Hasn't it, instead, given us a *full-fat society*, with tonnes of socio-economic cholesterol clogging the social body as every compartment of life is laboriously enlisted to make ends meet? Talk to any employee today about what their job entails and skill is usually only part of the picture. They also have to make friends with clients; join in with an obligatory after-work beer; ingratiate themselves to the line manager and attend horrific weekend picnics. This even extends to the instrumental use of social media. All these 'clingy' social pressures of neoliberal capitalism actually make Fordism look lean, trim and efficient in comparison, which is something of an achievement!

When picked up in the media, the quirky side of this trend is usually emphasized. For example, an online news forum recently asked readers: 'Do You Have to Avoid Huggers at Work?'[71] A woman with experience in healthcare and law enforcement said, 'Hugging was a huge part of my workplace, a huge part in maintaining these personal relationships.' Close human touch was 'a way to say to someone that you've made a connection with them, and that you trust them'. A similar news story reads, 'Is it Ever Appropriate to Sign Work Emails With an X?'[72] Yet another piece reveals how firms in London encourage alcohol consumption in the office, with 'booze trolleys' making an appearance on Friday afternoons.[73] All good fun.

But, as we saw with Zappos, Appco and the personal fitness instructors mentioned earlier, this personalization of economic activity has a dark side. The bureaucracy that California management gurus and neoliberal pundits want to scrap in the name of being 'more human' is often the employee's last line of defence when being harassed or unfairly targeted by an employer. Recall how *Reinventing Organizations* – the book that inspired Tony Hsieh at Zappos – said that flat organizations are the best way to inject soul back into the office. What isn't mentioned is that, in the human soul, an evil spirit may dwell – especially in a climate of economic brutalism, which rejoices in self-centredness and ruthless rivalry. This is why the French philosopher Gilles Deleuze once joked that the idea corporations have a soul is the most terrifying news in the world.[74] It isn't hard to see what he means when it comes to the morning after a particularly messy office party. Please tell me I didn't drink half a bottle of bourbon in front of our teetotalling Managing Director! Oh god, I didn't really say *that* to him, did I? What was supposed to be a shot of 'soul' turns out to be a hangover-mired nightmare – hence many employees will try to avoid these events like the plague.[75]

De-Raping the World of Work

This dark side runs deep. Take the practice of workplace hugging mentioned above. While the issue sounds awkward and rather light-hearted, there is a more sinister story here. A recent survey of women employed in the US fast-food industry found that 40 per cent had experienced unwanted sexual advances on the job.[76] Hugging and touching were frequently involved. Thousands of women were polled, and here is an itemized breakdown of the behaviour they reported:

Comments or questions about your gender or gender identity (9%)

Pressure to go out with someone (9%)

Requests for sex (8%)

Shown or received sexually explicit images (6%)

Someone rubbed their genitals against you (6%)

Told to flirt with customers (6%)

Told to alter your appearance beyond the restaurant's dress code, such as wearing tighter clothing or makeup (6%)

A person exposed parts of their body to you (5%)

Told to expose any part of your body (4%)

Asked to pose for or send nude photos (3%)

Offered more hours, a promotion, or any other benefit in exchange for a date or sexual favors (3%)

Sexually assaulted or raped (2%)[77]

What's surprising about the study is that most women say they hardly ever report the harassment to a supervisor. They try to deal with it themselves, using avoidance strategies, because they expect negative professional consequences if they openly accuse someone: 'Many workers feel that they are on their own when it comes to dealing with unwanted sexual behaviour at work, and they often resort to making personal sacrifices to avoid harassers.'[78]

Of course, not all forms of informality are as nefarious as this, and some may even act as a corrective to economic disenfranchisement in such environments.[79] My argument is simply this. With the rise of neoliberal capitalism as a totalizing economic paradigm, monetary formalism is often accompanied by a negative or inverse informalism, born out of state deregulation, the contraction of the public sphere and the hegemony of private individualism. Sexual harassment, bullying and excessive displays of power in the workplace are not an aberration from free market capitalism, but its dirty flipside. I think this is the true meaning of *economic privatization*. Whereas a strong public sphere once flushed out petty tyrants and bullies from the dark corners of organizational life, free-marketeers insist that you deal with it in a strictly private capacity. It's between you and the boss.

It may be recalled from chapter 2 that Hayek used the metaphor of a roadmap to justify free market individualism.[80] The state should only ensure the map is accurate, but never tell you where to drive. That's your choice. Similarly, apart from some very minimal legal requirements that are clear to all, the nature of the employment relationship ought to be determined only by the parties involved. To reveal the absurdity of Hayek's roadmap analogy, let's apply the same logic to a fire evacuation plan in a large hotel. The government should make sure that it's a sound representation of the premises, and nothing else. Although the plan identifies a suitable exit, no public authority should instruct people what to do in the event of a fire. That would be an infringement on their personal liberty. Guests are entirely free to act as they choose . . . perhaps escape out of a window, stay where they are or even set up a lemonade stand to turn a profit as everyone flees. Oh, and there will be no professional help available, of course. Publicly funded firefighters are inherently wasteful and (as argued in Public Choice Theory) generally driven only by their own self-interests, secretly benefitting from fires because they create work. A fire brigade constitutes a 'moral hazard' (like most of the welfare state), perversely incentivizing people to be careless in the kitchen because they assume someone will save them, no matter what. At the end of the day, guests are on their own, unless they pay for assistance privately, of course. But that's their business, since why should taxpayers subsidize complete strangers?

You get my point.

The example illustrates that a healthy and vibrant public sphere is often very compatible with individual self-interest (e.g., escaping a hotel fire), not anathema to it. So, rather than dismissing bureaucracies as lazy totalitarian monsters, I think we ought to champion *radical bureaucracies* instead. These organizations have a mission of public foresight and the enablement of personal freedom, exposing private interactions (e.g., between a female restaurant worker and her lascivious boss) to civic scrutiny. Pertaining to the workplace, this would mean disrupting the dichotomy that Hannah Arendt traced back to the ancient Greeks.[81] The household (i.e., *oikos*, or the economy, where the needs of biological self-preservation are met) tends to be private and rather unfree. We work or perish. Only when such economic survival is secured can we freely enter public life and speak our mind in the *polis* with confidence. Guaranteed material well-being promotes candid speech. But in the age of precarity and crippling power inequalities inside the *oikos*, such social confidence is in short supply. Most cannot speak openly in the workplace or beyond. Too much is kept private, especially in those encounters of egregious servitude. We're barred from sharing our collective experiences in any meaningful sense. As a result, the public sphere wilts and the *oikos* withdraws from the realm of legitimate debate, all but inscrutable to the law.

Isn't it time to unsettle the Arendtian formula – that is, to shine the light of public dialogue into the darkened world of work where innumerable travesties are rumoured to have taken place? Radical bureaucracies would reverse the gaze of state surveillance as it presently stands (where the powerful watch the disempowered), and instead expose the private *oikos* to democratic accountability and collective responsibility. And what could be more human than that?

Chapter Five

No More Buddy Buddy

Mike Judge's 1999 film *Office Space* is dreadful in many respects.[1] The plot wanders. The script is patchy. It relies on inaccurate stereotypes. Having said that, it's easy to see why most viewers (including myself) love the part where Jennifer Aniston's character – fast-food restaurant server Joanna – tells her overbearing boss to go fuck himself.

It all started weeks before. Exactly how much 'flair' (i.e., personal badges, pins and brooches) should Joanna attach to her Chotchkie's restaurant uniform? Company policy states a minimum fifteen pieces are required, which she complies with. But her supervisor Stan isn't happy. He wants Joanna to go the extra mile and embrace the spirit of the idea. Look at fellow-worker Brian, for example, who has thirty-seven pieces of flair and a 'wonderful smile'. Sure, fifteen might be the minimum, but great employees 'choose to wear more and we encourage that'. Finally, Stan gets to the point. He simply wants Joanna to express herself, allow customers to see her glowing personality. She mechanically nods in agreement. Following weeks of harassment, Joanna finally snaps:

Joanna: You know what, Stan, if you want me to wear 37 pieces of flair, like your pretty boy over there, Brian, why don't you make the minimum 37 pieces of flair?

Stan: Well, I thought I remembered you saying that you wanted to express yourself?

Joanna: You know what, I do want to express myself, okay [angrily flipping-off Stan who now holds his hands up as if Joanna is pointing a gun]. There's my flair, OK? And this is me expressing myself [and then flips-off the customers who similarly cower from the offensive weapon. Babies start to cry].

The sequence is satisfying – in an otherwise mawkish film – because the fantasy of exit is so *cleanly* fulfilled. Thoughts of an abrupt departure are fundamental to how we mentally cope with working in the dying economies of the West. This is not about actual exit, of course – simply its possibility, a symbolic gesture, no matter how remote and unrealistic.[2] The internal reasoning is straightforward: I can only tolerate this awful job if a sudden and extreme escape route is at least theoretically imaginable.

Perhaps the wish is popular today because (a) the conventional 'shock absorbers' between workers and their jobs (i.e., unions, workers' councils, collective contracts, etc.) have been considerably weakened, and (b) in our present work-obsessed culture, the individual is completely defined by what they do for a living. As a result, it creeps into everything, and we become our jobs. Whereas a factory worker left the role behind as they clocked out, the post-industrial proletariat live with it 24/7. And the demands that work makes on them become excruciatingly personal. The change is exemplified by employers wanting not just your labour time but soul or 'flair' too, as humorously depicted in *Office Space*.

One might think that this claustrophobic presence of work – where it actually gets under your skin – might promote an attitude of resignation and defeat. Since there is no longer any 'outside', all resistance is futile. But the ideological conditioning process is seldom complete.

It functions via a loose and fragmented structure rather than as a monolithic force. And we are given just enough agency – the tyranny of choice – to painfully recognize our predicament. That's why this asphyxiating sense of totality can fan dreams of a *final break*, as if working has become an endless existential prison that can only be escaped through wild acts of desperation.

The scene in *Office Space* captures the blurring of the formal-informal dualism that I've been focusing on in this book. All the qualities of an employee that ought to be personal are objectified and calibrated against some rather unforgiving metrics. But therein lies the paradox of deformalization. Employers cannot contractually oblige workers to feel a particular way since the doxa of 'choice' would disappear, and that is fundamental to capitalism. Joanna's flair is only useful to the firm if she *freely chooses* to express it. In reality, there is no choice, we know. She's being pressured by her boss. But it's this tension between self and non-self that reveals the underbelly of the 'free to choose' credendum essential to neoclassical economics. On the one hand, it requires people expressing their free will without duress, as they cannot be legally exploited otherwise (that would be slavery). And, on the other, workers who fear the dire economic consequences if they say 'no'. This we might call the *micro-fascism of choice* that now permeates late capitalism, typically enwrapped in the lexicon of personal liberty.

But isn't the supposed selfish individual at the heart of neoliberal mythology very different from the beaten figure we see in Joanna? Yes. However, an important metamorphosis has taken place in this regard. In his influential 1962 study of 'possessive individualism', C. B. Macpherson traces the contours of this persona, bequeathed to us as it was by the liberal philosophical tradition and then subsequently perfected by neoclassical economists and legalists:

its possessive quality is found in its conception of the individual as essentially the proprietor of his own person or capacities, owing nothing to society for them. The individual was seen neither as a moral whole, nor part of a larger social whole, but as an owner of himself.[3]

This character is a voracious *taker*, a person who refuses to entertain lasting bonds that otherwise underwrite our moral and social universe. From this perspective, other people are either useful stepping-stones or an impediment to economic self-optimization. Large swathes of mainstream economics adopt this image of man, developing notions of human capital theory, opportunity and transaction cost analysis, principal/agency theory, moral hazard and so forth. And a quick visit to the banking district in London or New York gives us some insight into what this obdurate ideal looks like when personified in the real world.

Nevertheless, something has changed in this respect. When the caricature of *Homo economicus* was translated into the concrete grammar of neoliberal capitalism over several generations, a different type of person slowly materialized – which might be dubbed a 'poor man's' individualism. It's still meant to be possessive and guided only by self-interest, of course. But, in reality, the subject has now become an object too, someone who is constantly *acted upon* by powerful institutions. To reiterate, the official emphasis is still on people seeking to possess things and others, but in reality he or she is mostly *dispossessed* – endlessly handing over crippling rents to live and work, ruthlessly judged (e.g., by customer ratings, student evaluations, etc.) and hounded in the process.

A Ruined Nation Awakens

Do Joanna's actions represent the future of resistance? No. Giving the finger to your boss and storming out won't halt the Uberization of dispossession currently unfolding in the workplace nor the micro-fascism of choice that tries to hold us captive. The only way to counter the horrible pressure of cash-intimacy is by collectivizing, of course. As opposed to Joanna's rebellious individualism, which is no doubt colourful and entertaining to watch, radical solidarity is grey and meticulous instead, and largely *external* to the individual personalities involved. That's what makes capitalism so afraid of it – there are no individual neuroses to hook into.

A new type of solidarity is emerging, which big business is endeavouring to crush. Recently, two Uber drivers in the UK – backed by the Independent Workers Union of Great Britain – won a court action in the British employment tribunal, claiming that London's 30,000 drivers had been misclassified. The tribunal agreed, a decision which was appealed by Uber.[4] In the appeal, the appellant – Uber Britannia – was again found liable:

> the reality of the situation was that the drivers were incorporated into the Uber business of providing transportation services, subject to arrangements and controls that pointed away from their working in business on their own account in a direct contractual relationship with the passenger each time they accepted a trip.[5]

While the ruling did not technically change their status as self-employed, it does mean the company must pay its drivers the minimum wage and provide holidays. Uber immediately appealed the decision once again. It's not giving up that easily.

The class action taken against Uber affecting 385,000 drivers in California and Massachusetts in 2016 provides another good example of workers attempting to *de-individualize* their jobs. Drivers claimed that their 'individual contractor' status was a misclassification. They're not independent 'driver partners' (as the firm calls them) because they have all the trappings of being a normal employee, except when it comes to pay and holidays. Moreover, drivers experience a great deal of management control that is enacted through app-regulated algorithms designed to exploit busy periods (i.e., keep drivers on the road). That level of influence should really only be present if a binding employment relationship is involved, a key test in employment law. As a rather critical report recently put it, 'Uber's self-proclaimed role as a connective intermediary belies the important employment structures and hierarchies that emerge through its software and interface design.'[6]

The ride-hailing giant faces having to make a massive pay-out if they lose the case. So, in 2016, Uber offered a US$100 million settlement to end the lawsuit.[7] This included a guarantee of US$84 million up front and an additional US$16 million conditional on future company earnings. Drivers and their representatives were keen to accept the offer. However, Judge Chen overseeing the case rejected the settlement in August 2016 as grossly unfair.[8] Taking into consideration both monetary and non-monetary relief, the proposed settlement 'yields less than 5% of the total verdict value of all claims being released'.[9] The total value was thought to be US$854 million.

Uber quickly realized its drivers had found a chink in the armour of platform capitalism – namely, banding together and challenging the company as a group in court, rather than as isolated individuals in private. As a stopgap solution to the rebellion, the company distributed a new 'driver partner agreement' in 2015.[10] It looks like an employment contract by any other name, of course, but legally it isn't. The document sought to *re-individualize* workers and stop them from pursuing collective litigation against the firm. Most significantly, in the event of any future disagreement, drivers must use a 'private dispute resolution process':[11]

15. 3. **IMPORTANT**: This Arbitration Provision will require you to resolve any claim that you may have against the Company or Uber on an individual basis . . . Except as provided below, this provision will preclude you from bringing any class, collective, or representative action . . . against the Company or Uber.

Unless the law requires otherwise, as determined by the Arbitrator based upon the circumstances presented, you will be required to split the cost of any arbitration with the Company.[12]

At the time of writing, all employees still have to sign the agreement, which would be legally problematic if it wasn't for an opt-out clause regarding the arbitration agreement. But, in true individualizing style, drivers must send a personal email (to optout@uber.com) stating their name and their individual wish to opt-out of provision 15.3.[13] Nothing like a little bit of psychological 'nudging' to help drivers make the 'right' choice and not send the email. The attorney representing the drivers in the lawsuit, Shannon Liss-Riordan, said, 'we believe this is an illegal attempt by Uber to usurp the court's role now in overseeing the process of who is included in the class'.[14]

Blog Warfare

Uber's efforts to undermine the ability of workers to collectivize captures the spirit of economic deformalization perfectly. The firm would rather deal with each driver individually on a personal basis. This isn't a new development at Uber. When Susan Fowler published a blog-post in February 2017 describing her year as an engineer at the company, we gained a rare insight into what it's like to work in an environment that lionizes unbridled individualism:

> On my first official day rotating on the team, my new manager sent me a string of messages over company chat. He was in an open relationship, he said, and his girlfriend was having an easy time finding new partners but he wasn't . . . he was looking for women to have sex with. It was clear that he was trying to get me to have sex with him, and it was so clearly out of line that I immediately took screenshots of these chat messages and reported him to HR.[15]

Fowler describes how she soon left the team and joined another. The culture she found there was also cut-throat, with managers undermining each other and vying for dominance. Taking a cue from other employees, she applied to be transferred to a less hostile department in the organization. Fowler was then told that 'my transfer was being blocked because I had undocumented performance problems'.[16] Undocumented? Officially, her performance was excellent. She kept pressing management for more information until a superior finally admitted, 'performance problems aren't always something that has to do with work, but sometimes can be about things outside of work or your personal life'.[17] Sadly, things only got worse from there, and Fowler quit.[18]

The story sparked much debate when it broke. Some said it even prompted CEO Travis Kalanick's resignation. The company was clearly toxic at almost every level. Views were varied on the subject, but *Wired* magazine asked the most incisive question: why aren't more workers *suing* Uber?[19] The reason why was discovered after talking to employees at the firm. The employment contract requires that all grievances be settled privately, by arbiters instead of a court and jury.

Despite such clauses riddling the industry and a major decline in union membership in most Western economies, alt-labour unions have started to have an impact. In the UK, for example, the Independent Workers Union of Great Britain has grown considerably, representing couriers and independent contractors. In the USA, groups like the New York Taxi Drivers Alliance have also made inroads into organizing New York's 45,000 Uber drivers, with minimum wage its central issue, since 'the bottom line is Uber destroys full-time work and replaces it with part-time poverty wages', according to a spokesman.[20]

How effective are these alt-labour unions?

In a perceptive analysis of the Deliveroo workers fighting for a better deal, Jamie Woodcock found that they were crucial and used a variety of innovative tactics.[21] In 2016, Deliveroo changed its policy of paying riders £1 per drop on top of a £7-an-hour wage to a flat rate of £3.75 per drop. That was the last straw and workers started to rebel. The very structure of the firm enabled them to collectivize. Whereas Uber drivers may never meet each other, Deliveroo operates in designated zones and riders are assigned waiting points near busy districts. Here they inevitably come into contact with each other and 'in the quieter periods drivers wait and chat together, providing the opportunity to begin collectively organising'.[22] These informal conversations developed into a conscious movement. In August 2016 riders assembled outside the Deliveroo London headquarters to voice their unhappiness. After the riders announced further action, the company backed down and abandoned the new policy.[23]

The act of collectivizing – involving a fluid street syndicalism – gave riders the power to protest openly. That's important, because they were then able to present the grievance in a public forum, enhancing the *visibility* of key issues. Most of the time, these workers aren't even registered by the firm, let alone anyone else. But now they were very 'visible outside, organising together, and angry'.[24] Moreover, the media and press arrived too. A piercing light was directed into the 'black box' of the gig economy so that all could see what was really going on. This went against the central ethos of platform capitalism and its love for covert, informal economic relationships. For what was meant to be an unofficial agreement was unceremoniously shoved into a public domain as throngs of workers gathered outside head office.[25]

The confrontation between budget airline Ryanair and its self-employed pilots in 2017 also demonstrates the power of alt-labour unions in action. For years, the firm has aggressively refused to negotiate with, or even recognize, trade unions. The stance didn't change when disgruntled pilots formed Ryanair Pilot Group to air their grievances. That was until the rebellion seriously threatened to damage the business. Was it a coincidence, for example, that pilots decided to take their annual leave *at the same time*, leaving the company without pilots during a busy period? After much pressure – including from other workers – CEO Michael O'Leary begrudgingly recognized the Ryanair Pilot Group accordingly.[26]

A key obstacle still remains for workers seeking to challenge Uberization – namely, the sizeable disconnect between their interests (e.g., as expressed by the Independent Workers Union of Great Britain) and those of employees in occupations threatened by platform capitalism. For example, in London, the Licensed Taxi Drivers Association is fairly hostile to Uber drivers and their representatives. If both unions could find common ground to form a united front, they'd be a formidable opponent. Of course, the fly in the ointment is the customer. When Transport for London refused to reissue Uber's London operating licence in 2017, over 400,000 people signed a petition to reverse the decision. Thus, any attempt to enlist Uber, Lyft and Deliveroo customers to the cause might be a difficult task. Imagine what could be achieved if these three integral stakeholders (i.e., Uberized workers, threatened non-Uberized workers and Uberized customers) were aligned (even loosely).

Robots Might Not Want Your Job

If building solidarity is the first port of call when it comes to opposing deformalization in and around the neoliberal enterprise, then skill and knowledge should probably be next. This is particularly salient in light of advancing digital technologies. There's been a great deal of talk about the impending jobless future that computerized automation will soon bring. But, despite the rapid rise of artificial intelligence, robotics and machine learning, it's surprising that *more jobs* haven't disappeared. In fact, unemployment rates in much of the Western world are comparatively low. There is a good reason why. Automation is guided by socio-economic forces (e.g., power) rather than its own intrinsic properties. For example, many companies don't believe it's *worth* automating certain jobs (such as cleaning, taxi-driving, etc.) because human labour available is already so cheap. With respect to Uber, it was only after 'driver partners' started to unionize and cause trouble that the company seriously began to consider driverless technology.[27] Other jobs simply cannot do without some human input. Take call-centres, for example. In the 1980s, it was predicted that they'd do away with most jobs in the service sector.[28] Today, millions are employed in call-centres. But the human component that remained was seriously deskilled, underpaid and precarious.

If automation won't necessarily abolish work, then it is significantly framing the deformalization of jobs. Three steps are involved.

First, digitalization separates the worker from the skill set required to undertake a job, but doesn't totally do away with the need for some human component *per se.*

Second, because the job now entails less expertise and attracts lower wages (since anyone can do it), the use of casualized labour and on-demand contracts are an easy option for employers. As we have learnt in previous chapters, this significantly deprofessionalizes an occupation and makes 'getting on' with the boss more important than it should be.

And third, the remaining qualities of the role become very social and subjective in nature. For example, senior managers in a call-centre understand that almost anyone can perform the technical side of the job. So their attention turns to the personal qualities of the workforce: an individual's attitude, enthusiasm and social affability. And such evaluations are frequently framed in very moral terms. Is he or she the 'right' person for the role?[29]

In their fascinating study of call-centre management in the UK, George Callaghan and Paul Thompson found that employee performance wasn't measured only in terms of how many calls were processed or how well, but the type of personality tele-agents expressed. It was considered an important indicator of customer service excellence.[30] This gave the work environment a very subjective and uncertain mood, because something like 'attitude' is difficult to quantify in any objective and neutral fashion. Personal bias creeps in. Just look at what one manager told his team:

> Some people are maybe not as fast round a keyboard, so they may struggle in achieving peer group average handling time for calls. But we can do something about that . . . Customer service. That's not a skill. That's in you. It's the attitude towards customer service. A positive attitude towards working and enjoy what you do.[31]

The same trend has been noted in other occupations, including airline pilots and lawyers. Automation doesn't destroy the work of junior lawyers, for example, but actively deprofessionalizes it. When a computer can process and check legal documents, the remaining human element is accordingly subcontracted out to an army of 'permatemps' who are underpaid and forced to draw on their own time and resources to get the job done, much like an Uber driver.

Robert Brooks demonstrates this in his study of freelancing attorneys in the USA.[32] Much of a junior attorney's labour process has been deskilled and semi-automated over the past few years, especially repetitive tasks like 'document review'. One temp who had trained for years to enter the profession said she was basically 'a glorified data entry person'.[33] The tension we've noted throughout this book was observable here, too. On the one hand, the job was extremely mechanistic and rationalized. Being paid by the hour meant every aspect of the work day was calculated and accounted for. On the other hand, a good deal of unpaid labour or prep-work outside formal hours was required, with an elaborate informal economy emerging behind the scenes as a result. In the office, strict authority structures mixed with casual informalism: 'well, the first day we were all in suits . . . but then, you know, you come in with more regular clothes'.[34] And then the abuse began. One temp remembers a senior partner storming into their office and yelling, 'you people in this rat hole!'[35] The workers had no choice but to suck it up.

Deskilling is really just a reflection of the unequal power relations that prevail in any given work situation or industry. It has little to do with technical innovation or the inevitable march of progress. Thus, to counter the deformalization that semi-automation can engender, skill has to be nurtured and protected among the workforce. One way to do this is to make jobs not worth automating from the employer's point of view – in terms not of cheap pay but of the strife that such an initiative would trigger. This brings us back to solidarity. A case in point is the London underground train service or 'Tube'. The National Union of Rail, Maritime and Transport (RMT) frequently strike, bringing the Tube to a painful standstill and chaos to the city. Officials have long promised to automate the system as a result (using Automatic Train Operation technology).[36] But, given the strength of the union and their indomitable bargaining position, the turmoil that would ensue clearly outweighs the long-term benefits of such an initiative – for now, at least.

None of what I am saying is a Luddite call to arms to smash the machines. Technology is great. But let's put the workers' perspective back into the debate. If robotics and AI are to obliterate all jobs, then we really do demand a luxurious utopia of leisure and play. However, if the institution of work is to remain in the 'second machine age', then the question of *worth* shouldn't be the sole preserve of employers (e.g., is this or that job worth automating?, etc.). Workers, too, ought to be able to decide whether a job *is worth doing*, in terms of the economic security it provides, the conditions under which it is performed and the creative enjoyment it permits. For this to happen, we would have to move beyond a society based solely on market individualism and the imperium of money, with policies like Universal Basic Income coming to the fore. A radical reclamation of technology would be essential too.

On Becoming a Monster

Solidarity and skill must now be set against a wider backdrop of the state, law and administrative bureaucracy, in terms of both political governance and individual workplaces. When used to rebuild society as a whole, the 'free market' experiment was by and large a socio-economic disaster. The details have been documented elsewhere and I will not repeat them here.[37]

Pertaining to our topic of interest, we've discovered that Hayekian legal formalism operates more like a smokescreen that hides a widening domain of private informality in the economy. Backroom deals are the order of the day. What were supposed to be 'more human' jobs – because they are liberated from red tape and more reliant on personal relationships – have often engendered episodes that wouldn't be out of place in *Lord of the Flies*. When the inequalities of power and income enter the picture, the line between being 'more human' and Nazi-like acts of inhumanity becomes frighteningly fine. Isn't this precisely the ambiguity that Brazilian novelist Clarice Lispector hit upon when she observed: 'who has not asked himself at some time or other: am I a monster or is this what it means to be a person?'[38]

I term this *over-humanization*: what arises when we get too much of the stuff, especially in numerical-fixated institutions that have a habit of turning fiscal restraint into a human zoo. We see this sometimes manifesting when pro-market governments view essential state services as business units or outsource them to corporate partners. Following

Hayek, the impersonal cash nexus is supposed to anonymize people, which is crucial if efficiency and due process are deemed paramount. Cash encourages emotional detachment, meaning that the dictum of *sine ira et studio* (without regard for persons) can be realized in undertaking public works. But that's not what happens on the ground, of course. As the regulatory gaze of qualitative (rather than just quantitative) accountability disappears – for this is now more of a private business matter – the informal sphere invariably expands, and anything can happen.

Look what occurred at Brook House Immigration Removal Centre located at London's Gatwick Airport, right next to the runway.[39] The service was outsourced to multinational firm G4S, who manage it as a profit-making enterprise. In August 2017, an alarmed employee secretly filmed what went on behind closed doors and leaked it to the media. The video revealed systemic chaos and incompetence, but also immigration officers 'mocking, abusing and even assaulting detainees'.[40] Clearly, the problem here wasn't the abundance of red tape and regulatory due diligence as Hayek and Steve Hilton would say, *but not enough*. We need to repossess legal formalism (i.e., statutory instruments, delegated legislation, regulatory law, etc.) and the concomitant organizational forms that articulate it – namely, the much-derided bureaucracy, and particularly its role in employment settings.

Two questions are important in this respect.

First, under present circumstances, is *new* legislation likely to appear that will extend the interests of the working majority and rebalance the power relationship that today inordinately favours employers? In terms of statutory law, that would mean relying on the political establishment to challenge the status quo, not to mention the emancipatory possibility of party/representative democracy. Some may be pessimistic about the prospects of this happening, or related avenues like judicial activism.

The second question pertains to *pre-existing* legal reason (together with precedent or common law) and whether it might be leveraged to curb the rampant exploitation in the gig economy and elsewhere. The Uber lawsuit in California mentioned above gives some hope. Workers first collectivized and then tapped into the same legal apparatus that has long facilitated the excessive individualization of work. And the ultimate outcome of this class action could very well send shock-waves throughout the platform economy and foster more enlightened employment practices.

Uberization of the Law?

There is a problem here, however. It concerns the relationship between the current configuration of the state, its semi-autonomous legal appa-ratuses and the potential for emancipatory change. Posed this way, we must ask the question: can we put our trust in a legal system (including the judiciary, the legislature, etc.) that's been so thoroughly neoliberal-ized over the last forty years?

We discussed earlier how the Chicago School of Law was pivotal in transforming legal reason and much jurisprudence into a battering-ram for big business. Conservative US legal scholars like Richard 'small-government-guy' Epstein have ceaselessly worked to make tort, tax law and property rights more favourable to the rich, reshaping the tenor of legal rationality in the process. Here is a sense of what we're dealing with. Epstein says he distrusts the very noun *capitalism* because it was probably invented by Karl Marx.[41] When criticizing Thomas Piketty's famous study of inequality and the compelling evidence he presented,

Epstein confessed: 'for my purposes I don't care if [the data] is true or false'.[42] And yes, he is one of the most influential legal scholars in the world.

This libertarian appropriation of jurisprudence has impacted on employment law throughout the OECD, casting doubt on the idea that courts are the best bet for advancing the interests of labour, despite recent case victories. The Uber lawsuit in California, for example, looks promising but (at the time of writing) is teetering on becoming a farce. Although Judge Chen ruled in favour of the litigants, a new legal struggle swiftly arose around whether drivers who didn't opt out of the arbitration clause could legally participate in the class action. A 2016 ruling by the Ninth Circuit Court of Appeals found that Judge Chen did not have the authority to assert that mandatory arbitration agreements (before the use of the class action opt-out waiver) are unenforceable. Therefore, drivers who either signed the original mandatory arbitration agreement or failed to opt out from the new agreement couldn't be involved in the class action. They will have to enter into private arbitration and challenge Uber alone.[43] In effect, this could potentially reduce the class action from many thousands of drivers to about 300. An appellate court will make a decision on that, although nobody knows when. Even if the class action is successful, and drivers are reimbursed for past expenses, the settlement will almost definitely require they continue to be classified as self-employed.

Or take the case of Californian Lyft-driver Patrick Cotter, who filed a nationwide class action against the San Francisco company in 2013. The suit was scaled back to include just 95,000 drivers in California. The action claimed the 'independent contractor' status was misleading, and the firm was liable for gasoline and maintenance expenses. Lyft's proposed settlement of US$12 million was rejected by US District Judge Vince Chhabria as well as alt-labour union Uber Lyft Teamsters

Rideshare Alliance, because it was a sizeable discount on potential total liabilities.[44] In April 2017, they settled by paying US$27 million instead. However, under the ruling, drivers are still to be classified as self-employed, with all the difficulties that this creates remaining unaltered.[45] As one observer coolly stated, 'It looks like Lyft got off fairly lightly here.'[46]

Another setback occurred in the case taken by workers against London Deliveroo in November 2017.[47] The Independent Workers Union of Great Britain argued that riders should be given the status of employees. No, said the judge, on the basis that the rider role was 'substitutable' and thus independent of Deliveroo, regardless of whether riders wear its uniform, ride exclusively for the company, and so forth. It was a controversial ruling, of course. One union official said that it assumed that 'because a rider can have a mate do a delivery for them, Deliveroo's low-paid workers are not entitled to basic protections'.[48]

The legal system has failed workers in other instances. For example, when the city of Seattle permitted Uber and Lyft workers to unionize, the ordinance was challenged by the US Federal Trade Commission and Department of Justice (backed by Uber, of course) via anti-trust legislation, particularly in relation to price-fixing.[49] Since drivers are independent business owners, unionization is tantamount to monopolistic collusion. The original US anti-trust laws, including the Sherman Act 1890 and Clayton Act 1914, exempted workers from anti-monopoly legislation, and for good reason.[50] That exemption has slowly been diluted, starting back in the 1940s with far-right thinkers such as Henry Simons and Fritz Machlup calling for trade unions to be included.[51] One early Chicago School economist – Frank Knight – even claimed: 'by far the worst monopolist restrictions are those organized by wage earners'.[52] Even back then, such statements were considered a little bizarre. Anti-trust legislation was designed to protect workers, consumers and small-business owners from gigantic conglomerates, not to serve them up on a platter. Unfortunately, the views of Frank Knight (filtered through the ideas of Hayek in particular) are now at the forefront of legal arguments on this topic, demonstrating how dire the situation is for gig economy workers.

One of the first principles of Western legality – *nulla poena sine lege*, or 'no penalty without the law' – has been abused by almost every ruling power since its adoption. How so? The decree essentially pivots on a temporal axis. Legislation cannot go back in time to criminalize behaviour that was once considered legal – or not considered at all. The logic is designed to protect those who engage in *non-instrumental (or unwitting)*, activities upon which the law hasn't yet deliberated, no matter how wrong the deed today. But what about the future? That becomes the post-legal hunting field where the new corporation prowls, territories unlegislated and ungoverned, and where *instrumental knowingness* reigns. Hence, in many respects, Uber and its cognates are innovators in post-legalism, with everyone else endeavouring to catch up.

The state allows this because, in much of the world, it is primarily a *capitalist state.*[53] It protects and advances the vested interests of the corporation almost automatically, mainly by disarming itself. Indeed, what first seem like legal victories often include conditions that retain the original fault (e.g., the self-employed classification), or worse. For example, in 2016 it was widely reported that France had drafted new laws that would protect workers from the tyranny of email and the encroaching e-demands of employers. The headlines spoke of work email being banned between the hours of 6 p.m. and 7 a.m.[54] But the reports concealed a rather bleaker reality. The law change merely allowed workers to *negotiate* email use with their employer, and thus marked an extension of the deformalization process we have been exploring. Hidden in the same set of legal reforms were clauses designed to make it easier for employers to dismiss workers. They didn't attract the same media hype as the 'French Firms Ban Email' story. When it comes to employees individually haggling over their 'right to disconnect', therefore, it isn't difficult to predict the outcome as the lone employee sits across from their disinterested boss, especially with unemployment hovering around the 10 per cent mark in France.

The Subtle Art of Giving a F**k

Rather than get bogged down in debates about the state and jurisprudence, perhaps it's better to start with the public sphere and build from there. We now know that market individualism operates as a Trojan Horse for privatizing social influence, replacing the *general* public executive with a *specific* boss who might like you today and hate you tomorrow. Money is its primary medium, but everywhere it is marked by social excess at the micro level (e.g., bullying, harassment), personal level (e.g., stress, anxiety) and the corporeal level (e.g., high blood pressure). The task we must set ourselves today is to fundamentally de-privatize the public sphere. For this to happen, an architecture of transparency must first be installed to connect an individual's particular circumstance to a generalizable set of norms of best practice. Under neoliberalism, that connection has been commandeered by the 'busybody state' and used to disenfranchise the individual.[55] Here the 'general intellect' – the bond that makes the fate of others (and especially their work) a shared concern for me too – is short- circuited. After that, I'm on my own ... as is everyone else – a collective isolation.

In light of the oppositional strategies outlined above, *radical bureaucracies* could reconnect the interests of the individual with those of the common, in an enabling (not coercive) manner, providing a framework for a sort of molecular solidarity of rights. When anyone mentions 'public goods' in the UK, images of vandalized telephone boxes are evoked (they are everywhere in London), providing a sort of telephonic rendition of the tragedy of the commons. If an asset or service isn't in private hands, the argument goes, then no one will care for it. This type of thinking is the product of a long ideological campaign to plant the golden axiom of private property at the heart of everything we do – even our sense of self. Radical or people's bureaucracies would seek to reverse this. They have five germane features for this purpose.

First, staff will be rewarded for *not* behaving like ruthless business managers, which is the opposite of what happens now. Underscored by a progressive taxation policy, these bureaux will have a mission to articulate the everyday practicalities of people-based ownership over essential institutional infrastructures. The notion that bureaucracies are bad because they're big is specious. Well-funded public organizations with a prominent civic charter are *way more* responsive, innovative and agile than the tired mega-corporations and dilapidated state bodies presiding over society today. Radical bureaucracies will have a strong social purpose (as described in chapter 3 in relation to fire regulations), and their legal code will reflect this. According to Hayek, that's dangerous, because once 'public opinion' enters the fray, government officers become partisan and biased.[56] In short, the economy is politicized. But the very phrasing of this argument assumes that the public is *already separated* from the administration of life and its democratic forms. That very fissure ends up personalizing politics, allowing the economy to get under your skin, as we've already noted. Moreover, with respect to Hayek's worry about certain agendas influencing governments and rendering its actions arbitrary, isn't this precisely what occurs now, only in the interests of the 1 percenters?

Second, these public organizations will be intrinsically democratic and accountable. The long dirty war that has been waged to discredit public institutions has to be countered. Yes, we need to be vigilant regarding any authoritarian tendencies. Otherwise – and as Max Weber observed long ago – there's a danger that only the governed are levelled by bureaucracy, 'in opposition to the ruling and bureaucratically articulated group, which in its turn may occupy a quite aristocratic position'.[57] No doubt this might occur, but it's not inevitable. As I mentioned earlier, it was actually Weber's student Robert Michels who inaugurated the incredibly conservative viewpoint that bureaucracies *always* end up dictatorial, no matter what we do.[58] When this message was filtered through Public Choice Theory, for example, neoliberalism found a rationale to downsize the state and promote capitalist individualism instead.[59] But isn't this a very cynical view of how public servants behave – namely, as self-serving power-grabbers? Economist Amartya Sen uses an imaginary scenario to demonstrate how neoclassical economists like James M. Buchanan see the world.[60] A stranger is visiting a new town and asks a local if he can direct him to the train station. 'Certainly', says the local and points in the opposite direction, towards the post office, asking, 'And would you mind posting this letter for me on the way?' 'Sure', says the departing stranger, resolving to open it as soon as possible to see whether it contains anything worth stealing.

Third, we ought to reject thoroughly the myth that the public organizations are old-fashioned, technologically inept and culturally grey or uncreative. They can be like that – usually following a round of budget cuts by free market politicians who have killed the collective mission of the enterprise (e.g., the Environmental Protection Agency in the USA where 'morale has plummeted, anxiety is rife, science is being choked off, and much work has been paralyzed').[61] But the facts speak for themselves. Some of the most innovative and path-breaking inventions stem from the 'entrepreneurial state' and the dynamism of public investment.[62] Indeed, if you want to see where innovation has actually stalled, then the corporate sector probably provides more illustrative examples. Don't be fooled by the glitz of Facebook or the iPhone. Back in the 1960s and 1970s, everyone imagined that 2018 would be a futurist dreamland, with robotics liberating humanity from toil and misery. But we got 'Dandy Dungeon' video games instead, and not flying cars or democratized medicine. As David Graeber laments, contemporary reality has turned out to be a beta-version of that science fiction fantasy.[63] That's mainly due to the grip that the corporate complex has on investment, and a penny-pinching state that bows to the market forces.

The fourth feature concerns how we fund people's bureaucracies. Where will all the money come from? Here the engineers of fiscal austerity have cultivated a big misperception – that state finances are analogous to household budgets. They aren't.[64] Governments that choose to run a budget surplus – the credo of capitalist austerity – are simply extracting *more* money from the community than they give back. In other words, government surpluses generally create private debt, which is where your credit card comes into the picture. What's more, governments can actually create money, issue bonds and draw on central bank mechanisms (e.g., quantitative easing). You and I can't at home.[65] What is for them an endless abstraction is for us a very finite resource, and it's been specifically designed that way. Money thus remains a great mystifier, especially when couched in dubious (and failed) theories such as expansionary fiscal contraction. Anyhow, public spending is an investment in the future rather than a drain on resources. This investment engenders the conditions that allow superior innovation and productivity to flourish in the first place. Once we dispel the 'balanced budget' myth, then a Universal Basic Income becomes viable, for example, which can be less expensive than punitive welfare. Radical bureaucracies are easily fundable in a manner that will create cascading social goods and representative inclusivity.

And, finally, it's obvious that jobs and employment will look very different in a context defined by radical or people's bureaucracies. Work will be governed by norms of a quasi-public character. The micro-fascism of choice that has privatized our entire existence will be negated. Thus, the act of de-privatizing the public sphere also invites us to rethink seriously what *human freedom* – and perhaps even *humanity itself* – actually means. Years of neoclassical economic dogma have water-boarded us into believing that freedom is a strictly private, individualistic affair.[66] Bureaucracy – and perhaps even society itself (which Maggie Thatcher said was an illusory concept) – smothers personal choice, difference and free will. I will demonstrate how we can think otherwise in the conclusion.

Conclusion

Less Human

Imagine a world in which everybody rented their house on Airbnb. The majority of workers are trapped in zero-hours contracts, on-call 24/7 with no sick leave or holiday pay. All car owners are Uber drivers too, incessantly rated by each other. Consider a society where personal connections alone determined your success on the job market, populated by Weinsteinian bosses at every turn who're only too happy to lend a helping hand . . . as long as you give them a little 'something' in return. A world where private individualism is practised to the nth degree and the public sphere is non-existent. No governmental protections. Few regulatory standards. Little democratic accountability.

Is that our future?

The contemporary socio-economic order is certainly in a bad way. But what's more worrying is that the trends discussed in this book haven't fully played out yet. Things could get much worse if corrective measures are not taken.

One reason for this has to do with the foundations of neoclassical economics. F. A. Hayek and Milton Friedman, for example, were essentially utopian thinkers, constructing abstract and theoretical worlds that looked perfect on paper, but were impossible to realize in practice.[1] As with other variants of utopianism, failure to fulfil the golden dream (of free market individualism in this case) is no deterrent. True believers simply try harder . . . over and over again. The worrying part is that a Hayekian utopia features few *actual* people . . . it is literally a 'no place'. Just look at the econometric equations and theorems that have flowed in the wake of the Chicago School. Real living and breathing human beings are almost an inconvenience.

So what transpires when this *people-less* doctrine is deployed to manage concrete, real-life workplaces? The utopia swiftly morphs into something rather ghostly, of course. A recent restructuring plan announced by UBS (a major European investment bank) gives some insight into what a Hayekian vision – with all its emphasis on anonymity, free agents and private individualism – looks like in practice.[2] The title of the *New York Times* report says it all: 'No Laptop, No Phone, No Desk'.

Whereas desk space in most office settings is inevitably 'possessed' by individual workers over time, cluttered with family photographs, chopsticks and kid's paintings for instance, senior managers at UBS are going for something different. The redesigned environment would be entirely transactional and peripatetic, with none of the social invest-ments we'd normally expect when people come together on a regular basis. Employees will have no allocated desks. They'd wear headsets rather than use handset phones. They can log on to the company system anywhere and aren't bound to the office locale. Nothing is fixed or rou-tine. This is an individual ethos that eschews static group norms. People still work together on projects but in an incessantly ad hoc, unpredict-able way – just like independent contractors. A managing director at UBS explained the new policy: 'being chained to a desk in a singular environment is restrictive'.[3] Another said that staff benefit from:

> working together, talking to each other, working in a more agile way. People are probably not so fixed any more in their working environment.[4]

Clearly, Hayek would have approved. This complements his extreme picture of how the economy should function, in that people never socially ossify or settle into classifiable collectives. Instead, they behave as autonomous (yet interactional) monads, moving to where the next market opportunity lies, consummately transactional, and displaying little interest in anything else. As we learn from Hayek's *The Road to Serfdom*, in the realm of commerce there can be no homelike certitudes or communal bonds.[5] Human solidarity is inefficient and sooner or later leads to totalitarianism.

However, therein lies the rub. Hayek's unrealistic utopia of perfect cash-anonymity has some very human consequences in real life. Sure, his arguments helped isolate the employee and render him/her imperceptible to the regulatory gaze of the state. But is the average employer and employee invisible to each other as a result? No – the opposite, in fact. This is not a story about desocialization, as some critics of neoliberal capitalism have argued, but a major recalibration of what the social means. The worst facets of the wider social structure are pushed onto individual actors to deal with alone (e.g., debt, stress, depression, divorce, etc.). Conversely, the best of the individual and his/her élan is swiftly sucked away by the same heartless structure, leaving them dry and empty . . . a non-person. Indeed, when I first read the article on UBS, I imagined a vast office space that had been emptied of human beings, leaving only a haunting husk of nothingness.

It's not surprising that this notional *disappearing* of the worker in neoclassical economics correlates with their concrete elimination in reality. 'Zero-hours' contracts have a rather sinister connotation in this respect. Take the tragic case of Don Lane, a 'self-employed' courier for parcel giant DPD.[6] Having been diagnosed with diabetes, he couldn't seek proper treatment because the company fined him £150 per day if a replacement wasn't found. After collapsing several times at the wheel, Lane's condition steadily deteriorated. He died in January 2018 having worked at DPD for nineteen years. The company's brutal employment system is highly financialized and impersonal, and in it drivers are nothing more than figures on a cold spreadsheet . . . a kind of labour-less utopia from DPD's perspective. Yet Don Lane 'lived' that very same system as a deeply personal and dystopic trauma. The broader cultural code of 'lean management' was ultimately carried by Lane's body, which soon succumbed and vanished.

How to Die on the Inside

It's within the social space cleared by the disjuncture between (a) impersonal, calculative commercialism, and (b) the renewed importance of privatized informalism, that we now see debates raging about what makes us human – for pro-capitalists and second-generation neoliberals who want to give this cash-universe a human face ascribe a symbiosis between money and selfhood, sovereign individualism and business enterprise. Steve Hilton typifies this in his book *More Human*.[7] Burn pointless red tape and significantly scale down the state. Only then can a more human approach to jobs and education be prepared, one in which people express their innate entrepreneurial qualities.

At the heart of Hilton's argument is the self-reliant individual. They bake their own bread in the South of France and found new start-ups in Silicon Valley. Business is in their DNA: 'To believe that you can do better than what's out there at the moment, to believe you can persuade other people to buy it from you, to believe it's worth taking a risk with your money in order to start a business, that is the uniquely human thing to do.'[8] This is how Hilton reduces the rich and complex history of Western humanism – stretching from the Renaissance and

Erasmus to the fecund intricacies of J. W. Goethe – to a mere sales pitch.

A similar sentiment is extended in Daniel Pink's insipid bestseller *To Sell Is Human*.[9] Like it or not, Pink argues, we're all in sales now. People today are always seeking to influence others and convince them to do something for them. Our very sociality – which is clearly an innate human trait – is geared around persuading others to act to serve our interests: to like your Facebook post; grant you a pay rise; give you a bank loan; go out on a date; do the laundry. This perpetual sales activity is not denominated in money, according to Pink, but time, attention and effort, and is thus an integral part of everyday life.

Is this a screwed-up proposition? Undoubtedly. But why? Well, first, there's the laughable attempt to try and infer that capitalism is at the heart of human nature. Pink's formulation runs like this: *to be human = to be social = persuading others to want what you have = sales*. In short, we are all natural-born capitalists. He then summarizes his argument:

> Selling, I've grown to understand, is more important, is more urgent, and, in its own sweet way, more beautiful than we realize. The ability to move others to exchange what they have for what we have is crucial to our survival and our happiness. It has helped our species evolve, lifted our living standards, and enhanced our daily lives. The ability to sell isn't some unnatural adaptation to the merciless world of commerce. It is part of who we are ... selling is fundamentally human.[10]

The argument conflates *any* type of human activity (which could just as easily include child abuse and genocide) with ontological traits that we all must share. Sorry. I'm neither an entrepreneur nor a salesman. Now let's flip the conceit upside-down for a moment and look at those who genuinely do see capitalism as an instinctive calling. Don't they present a rather lame example of human nature in light of the 2007–8 banking debacle?

Almost Human . . . Almost

A glaring problem arises at this point. There's no theory of the *inhuman* in any of these fashionable arguments. Economic mistreatment, bullying, hazing rituals and sexual assault? No, the mawkish humanism promoted by second-generation neoliberals ignores the nasty side of our nature. Interestingly, Pink comes fairly close to acknowledging these more troubling qualities when describing why some audiences dislike his argument: 'they have this association that sales is sleazy, slimy, smarmy, lowbrow, it's about hoodwinkery and sleezebaggery'.[11] But it's not.

Hasn't Pink inadvertently hit the nail on the head here?

In deconstructing this nouveau libertarian humanism, it's not enough to resort to Hobbes like everyone else . . . people are born violent wolves and require the state to tame them. As Gilles Deleuze pointed out, the state doesn't really work in this manner and neither does human desire. Deleuze is often seen as the poster-boy of optimistic postmodernism and joyful Spinozian ethics, but he was in fact quite pessimistic about human beings.[12] Some kind of inhumanity is never far away, yet we constantly misunderstand it as an ethical malfunction or aberration. However, wickedness can only materialize in an act of agency, a person's capacity to choose otherwise. And agency is part of our nature. That's why cats, dolphins and elephants have no place here, since only people can be really evil.[13]

Matters are much worse than this, however, according to Deleuze.

It's not just the abominable way people treat others that disturbed him about humans. No, he discovered something even more sinister; often, we feel most human precisely when *we're* the ones being treated like dirt.[14] Humiliation and pain typically scramble the sensibilities of non-human animals, but not us. It can make us feel whole again. Total negation awakens something complete and final. And that's an alarming revelation for many reasons, none of which inspires much confidence in the human race, including interactions of the most ordinary kind: 'encounters with people are always catastrophic'.[15]

On a more positive note, what about the radical and often complicated humanism that is promoted on the left? Noam Chomsky, for example, has long maintained that we have a natural inclination towards spontaneous cooperation, free production and creative sharing. Therefore, we must work to bring about better institutions – anarcho-syndicalism – to complement our nature, not smother it as capitalist culture does.[16] According to Chomsky, big progress has been made in this direction in Western societies.[17]

More recently, David Harvey has made the case for *secular revolutionary humanism*, claiming it could dovetail with liberation theologies that have been so popular among the working class: mainly Catholicism and Protestantism. He understandably chooses to omit Islamic variants of radical spirituality emerging in the Wahhabi and Salafist doctrines.[18] Within the Western paradigm at least, Harvey's revolutionary humanism is 'very different to bourgeois humanism. It refuses the idea that there is an unchanging or pre-given "essence" of what it means to be human and forces us to think hard about how to become a new kind of human.'[19]

Harvey's anti-capitalist verve is admirable, as well as arguments in a similar vein, including 'dark ecology' in particular.[20] But I still believe that the focus on 'being human' is a red herring. In relation to the topic of this book, it risks fetishizing or decontextualizing what is in fact a socio-political problem. Perhaps it's better to start from the other end of the spectrum and begin with public organizational forms, with few guarantees they will evince morally 'correct' people.

People's Bureaucracies to Come

A radically reinvigorated public sphere is probably the only way we can halt and reverse the Hayekian dystopia that turned late modernity into an intolerable quagmire. This is particularly so in relation to the deformalization movement, the illegitimate offspring of neoclassical economics.

Before we summarize the basic principles of people's bureaucracies, a caveat is first required. One tactic that the establishment deploys today in order to undermine criticism is to ask a simple question: what's your alternative? It's almost as if we're expected to unroll a large blueprint of a new society, in which everything has its place down to the last detail. But here is the catch. If you do have such a blueprint, then you're immediately dismissed as a megalomaniac Stalinist or an unrealistic dreamer. And if you don't have a blueprint, you are dismissed for not having anything better to replace the status quo with. The question is a trap. To avoid this double bind, it makes more sense to turn the argument around and place the onus on the economic/political elite instead. That's what the Black Lives movement did in the USA recently when opposing police violence. One placard read: 'What's the alternative? Stop shooting us' – a simple demand. And eminently realistic. Similarly, rather than be summoned by the authorities to present a fully fledged template of a new social order (which I'm certainly not qualified to provide), our first demand ought to be this: the ongoing economic brutalization of the population has to stop – very workable and very achievable ... right now.

Once collective self-protection is obtained for the unemployed, the working poor and the growing numbers of the middle class crippled by debt and useless work, then a number of highly democratic and progressive interventions could be proposed. Over the course of this book, we've discussed four ideas regarding how we might curb the trend of deformalization underlying the neoliberal crisis. These can be summarized as follows.

Nullify economic desperation The main reason people put up with the vagaries of what might be called a dark intra-economy (i.e., informal, arbitrary, etc.), presently functioning in the shadows of neoliberal capitalism, is because *they have to*. There is little choice, since failure to ingratiate yourself to a boss, feign docility or go along with the harassment could lead to destitution. *Fear* is the chief emotional currency of the neoliberal deformalization movement. As a result, it's easy to see why more powerful parties can get away with all sorts of intrusions into the lives of subordinates, including close encounters of the Weinsteinian kind.

If we nullified that deep-seated insecurity – with a Universal Basic Income, for example – then people would be less willing to endure poisonous employment conditions quietly. Such a policy would actually cost the public purse less, because the expensive infrastructure of the 'unemployment industry' would no longer be required. Nor would the indirect subsidies (e.g., tax breaks, food stamps, housing benefits, etc.) that are used to support those employers who refuse to pay their workers properly. While no panacea, a Universal Basic Income could certainly do its part to cultivate a much more civilized and human-compatible economic system.[21]

Outlaw sham self-employment and zero-hours contracts The individualization of work and the precipitous rise of *Homo contractus* was sold to us as a path to freedom. Under so-called 'flexible' work systems, we get to call the shots and choose how to work. That promise turned out to be a bad joke, since the exact opposite has happened. Most businesses use self-employment contracts simply to offload the costs of work onto the 'employee' and treat them as economic playthings. No wonder that this *flexploitation* can make life so unnecessarily stressful, transferring complete control to the employer. That power relationship needs to be rebalanced by legislating against this development, something that's starting to occur with on-demand or 'zero-hours' contracts.[22] I'm not saying that genuine self-employment doesn't exist. It does in all sorts of situations, especially outside the metropolis. But the principle should not be abused to disempower what are *de facto* employees. If governments don't act to reverse this, then employees will, as we've recently seen in a number of high-profile campaigns.[23]

De-privatize the public sphere We need a renewed public sphere that can provide scrutiny and security in our economic affairs, particularly in relation to labour standards, consumer safety and tax law. Radical bureaucracies would take the best of the modern administrative ethos and blend it with a social mission of civic enablement rather than alienation. What's more, tax law and the legal underpinnings of employment contracts must be thoroughly de-individualized to allow collective voice and economic equality. Work and employment could easily be de-privatized too in this manner, safeguarding due process and public transparency, smoking out the private despotism that can take hold when employers regulate themselves. Moreover, unlike the dire predictions about the 'iron law of oligarchy', people's bureaucracies would be horizontally ori-entated (or molecular) instead of what we have now – tall pyramids out of touch with ordinary citizens. Federations could reorder the division of labour in an egalitarian manner whereby formal justice is publicly observed. Only then can we let our individuality shine rather than huddle in fear.

De-centre the institution of work Work has been highly defor-malized with the advent of the 'gig economy', Uberization and the massive campaign to transform the workforce into lone individu-als. Moreover, a backdrop of fierce socio-economic inequality has exacerbated the tendency, pushing the labour/capital relationship underground in many respects. Three things are clearly wrong with the world of work today. First, having a job is too often a path *into* economic insecurity rather than out of it.[24] Jobs need to be made more secure with less hellish and humiliating terms and conditions. A Universal Basic Income, banning zero-hours contracts, and civic providence by radical bureaucracies will help there. Second, despite all the talk about free market individualism and liberation man-agement among neoliberal ideologues, most workplaces are now governed by staunchly undemocratic, authoritarian hierarchies. It's ironic. Research has discovered that so-called 'flexible' work systems end up attracting way more top-heavy management struc-tures than other jobs.[25] This veritable explosion of managerialism has helped fuel perverse levels of pay inequality as organizational elites detach themselves from the rest of society. In the USA, for example, the CEO-to-worker compensation ratio was 20:1 in 1965. In 2014, it stood at 299:1.[26] Add stock options to the mix and the ratio is probably even worse. CEO salaries need to be capped (or at least put to employee vote using 'participatory budgeting' mechanisms), and workers' councils given direct involvement in both strategic and operational decision-making. Worker-controlled co-operatives and partnerships can play a major role here.[27] And, third, *fewer* people are now working *more*. Therefore, jobs need to be more evenly distributed across the economy and less of it done by individuals on average, moving towards a three-day work week, which the mounting evidence suggests will lead to more productivity, not less.[28]

There are two further points that can be made in conclusion.

The deformalization movement – in all its variants – is a product of an ideology gone very wrong, namely neoclassical (and now mainstream) economics. Hayek's and Friedman's pontifications about free market individualism and unbridled capitalism have helped to engender a nightmarish situation in which many are desperate, totally dependent on employers and often broke to boot. As mentioned in the book's introduction, we can see a red thread connecting Hayekian economic privatism and the dirty world of Harvey Weinstein preying on young women – for deregulation really means power obtaining licence to do what it wants. I agree with ultra-conservative legalists like US jurist Richard Epstein that the employment relationship needs to *be unlocked,* using his words.[29] But he meant unlocked from the state and statutory protections so that wages can be determined by market forces and private negotiation. His defence of at-will contracts in US employment law – where workers can be dismissed at any time without just cause, simply because the boss feels like it – is indicative of where this line of reasoning leads: the return of an unregulated nineteenth-century 'Wild West' variant of capitalism.[30] Whereas I mean the opposite: *publicly unlocking* the murky relationship that a part-time worker gets trapped in, alone and super-reliant on a supervisor who feels free to pinch her arse 'at will'. As the numerous examples described in this book indicate, this is where capitalist libertarianism ultimately leads. So it is really time to consign this brand of economics to the dustbin of history and develop less sleazy models.

And finally, it is clear we need to question the current rendition of personal freedom as it has been forged by Chicago School economists and subsequently diffused in most institutions we live in and around today. The so-called 'freedom to choose' that Hayek and Friedman glorified has in reality turned to shit. This is probably because the argument was more of an excuse to try and kill off collective organizational forms (unions) and norms (labour law and standards) that stood behind the worker in the past and fought their corner. Now those countervailing forces are weakened, workers are increasingly on their own. The lesson from this is obvious. Without the freedom to debate and influence the socio-political backdrop that prefigures the options presented to me, there simply can be no proper personal freedom. It only comes from collective solidarity and the concomitant freedom to step back and walk away from any given social situation. This is sometimes called *flexicurity*.

Neoclassical economics tried to pit the individual against society and its organizations, construing the community as an impediment to the liberty we crave. The more we are separated from each other, the freer we are meant to be. While the idea is ludicrous for many reasons, it has fundamentally captured the institutional logics that shape our world, even in the face of the monumental failures and pervasive economic hardship. The endgame of this dark fantasy is now approaching. The ideological spell has been broken. We cannot truly express our individuality and personal freedom as capsule-like lone wolves – unless you're independently wealthy that is, in which case nothing I've said really matters . . . yet.

Notes

Introduction: The Economics of Sleaze

1   J. Kantor and M. Twohey (2017). 'Harvey Weinstein Paid Off Sexual Harassment Accusers for Decades'. *The New York Times*. Available at https://www.nytimes.com/2017/10/05/us/harvey-weinstein-harassment-allegations.html.

2   S. Levin (2017). 'Ex-Weinstein Staffer Says Assistants Were Manipulated: "We Weren't Safe Either"'. *The Guardian*. Available at https://www.theguardian.com/film/2017/oct/17/ex-weinstein-staffer-says-assistants-were-manipulated-we-werent-safe-either.

3   A. Quart (2017). 'What's the Common Denominator among Sexual Harassers? Too Often, It's Money'. *The Guardian*. Available at https://www.theguardian.com/us-news/2017/nov/09/sexual-harassment-economic-inequality-harvey-weinstein.

4   G. Hinsliff (2017). 'How Harvey Weinstein's Accusers Gave Women Worldwide a Voice'. *The Guardian*. Available at https://www.theguardian.com/society/2017/oct/21/harvey-weinstein-accusers-women-voice-sexual-abuse.

5   E. Nyran (2017). 'Harvey Weinstein Intern Alleges He Harassed Her in 1980'. *Variety*. Available at http://variety.com/2017/film/news/harvey-weinstein-intern-sexual-harassment-1980-1202590582; Levin, 'Ex-Weinstein Staffer Says Assistants Were Manipulated'.

6   *The New Yorker* (2017). 'Statement from Members of the Weinstein Company Staff'. Available at https://www.newyorker.com/news/

news-desk/statement-from-members-of-the-weinstein-comp
any-staff.

7 R. Farrow (2017). 'Harvey Weinstein's Army of Spies'. *The New Yorker.* Available at https://www.newyorker.com/news/news-desk/harvey-weinsteins-army-of-spies.

8 B. Marling (2017). 'Harvey Weinstein and the Economics of Consent'. *The Atlantic.* Available at https://www.theatlantic.com/amp/article/543618.

9 H. Stewart and P. Walker (2017). 'Theresa May to Crack Down as Sex Harassment Allegations Grow'. *The Guardian.* Available at https://www.theguardian.com/politics/2017/oct/29/theresa-may-to-crack-down-as-sex-harassment-allegations-grow.

10 C. Farand (2017). 'Tory Minister "Admits Making Aide Buy Sex Toys Amid Westminster Harassment Scandal"'. *The Independent.* Available at www.independent.co.uk/news/uk/politics/stephen-crabb-mark-garnier-westminster-harassment-claims-sex-toy-text-messages-a8025351.html.

11 Stewart and Walker, 'Theresa May to Crack Down as Sex Harassment Allegations Grow'.

12 Hayek calls this capitalist utopia of anonymous, spontaneous order, the 'Great Society': F. A. Hayek (1973). *Law, Legislation and Liberty: A New Statement of the Liberal Principles of Justice and Political Economy.* London: Routledge and Kegan Paul, p. 6.

13 For example, see R. Solnit (2010). *A Paradise Built in Hell: The Extraordinary Communities That Arise in Disaster.* New York: Penguin. Also see P. Clastres (1989). *Society Against the State: Essays in Political Anthropology.* New York: Zone Books; J. C. Scott (2014). *Two Cheers for Anarchism: Six Easy Pieces on Autonomy, Dignity, and Meaningful Work and Play.* Princeton University Press.

14 F. A. Hayek (1944). *The Road to Serfdom.* London: Routledge. Hayek clearly borrows this claim from his mentor, Ludwig Von Mises, who stated 'it is impossible to grasp the meaning of the idea of sound money if one does not realize that it was devised as an instrument for the protection of civil liberties against despotic inroads on the part of government. Ideologically it belongs in the

same class with political constitutions and bills of rights': L. von Mises (1912/1953). *The Theory of Money and Credit*. New Haven: Yale University Press, p. 414.

15 Hayek, *The Road to Serfdom*; F. A. Hayek (1960). *The Constitution of Liberty*. University of Chicago Press.

16 D. Sperber and H. Mercier (2017). *The Enigma of Reason: A New Theory of Human Understanding*. London: Allen Lane.

17 See S. Mullainathan and E. Sharif (2013). *Scarcity: Why Having too Little Means So Much*. New York: Henry Holt & Company.

18 R. Tweedy (2017). 'A Mad World: Capitalism and the Rise of Mental Illness'. *Red Pepper*. Available at https://www.redpepper. org.uk/a-mad-world-capitalism-and-the-rise-of-mental-illness.

19 F. Berardi (2011). *After the Future*. Oakland, CA: AK Press, p. 90.

20 See S. Hill (2017). *Raw Deal: How the 'Uber Economy' and Runaway Capitalism Are Screwing American Workers*. New York: St Martin's Press.

21 This is one explanation for the recent resurgence of populism – not as a rejection of neoliberalism but as a mutation or extension of it. Nationalists find fertile ground following mass marketization, since increasing numbers are disenfranchised and without the progressive generalizations that once countered the mythology of capitalism. In the era of Trump and Brexit, therefore, money remains a universal motivator, only its damaging effects are displaced away from 'capitalism' and onto immigrants and ethnic minorities instead. This is why fascism and neoclassical economics can closely coexist.

22 For example, when celebrating 'independent' workers compared to regular employees, Hayek states, 'for the independent there can be no sharp distinction between his private and his business life, as there is for the employed, who has sold part of his time for a fixed income'. See Hayek, *The Constitution of Liberty*, p. 188.

23 As former CEO Travis Kalanick put it, 'Uber began life as a black car service for 100 friends in San Francisco – everyone's private driver. Today we're a transportation network spanning 400 cities in 68 countries that delivers food and packages, as well as people, all at the push of a button.' See T. Kalanick (2016). 'Celebrating

Cities: A New Look and Feel for Uber'. Available at https://www.uber.com/newsroom/celebrating-cities-a-new-look-and-feel-for-uber-7.

24 For example, 50 per cent of all jobs created in the OECD since 1995 are of this non-standard insecure type: OECD (2015). *In It Together: Why Less Inequality Benefits All.* Paris: OECD Publishing, p. 29. In the UK, the number of people employed on 'zero-hours contracts' in December 2015 was 804,000. That figure grew to 1.4 million in May 2017: Office for National Statistics (2018). 'Contracts That Do Not Guarantee a Minimum Number of Hours: September 2017'. Available at https://www.ons.gov.uk/employmentandlabourmarket/peopleinwork/earningsandworkinghours/articles/contractsthatdonotguaranteeaminimumnumberofhours/september2017.

Moreover, official employment and unemployment figures can be misleading as to the true structure of the labour market, mainly because governments only count those 'actively seeking work' as unemployed. By this reckoning (as of December 2017), there are 32 million employed and 1.4 million unemployed in the UK. Missing here are the *economically inactive.* Once we subtract retirees, the number of 16- to 64-year-olds falling into this category is 8.7 million (or a quarter of the eligible workforce). This represents a massive 'black hole' in the economy. How do these people make ends meet? One can only infer that 'ghost jobs' are rife. Office for National Statistics (2018). 'UK Labour Market: February 2018'. https://www.ons.gov.uk/employmentandlabourmarket/peopleinwork/employmentandemployeetypes/bulletins/uklabourmarket/latest#summary-of-latest-labour-market-statistics.

25 B. Balaram and F. Wallace-Stephens (2018). 'Are British Workers Thriving, Striving, or Just about Surviving?' *Royal Society of Arts.* Available at https://www.thersa.org/discover/publications-and-articles/reports/seven-portraits-of-economic-security-and-modern-work-in-the-uk.

26 In an excellent article, Laurent Derobert shows this in neoclassical labour-supply models, particularly those developed by Philip Wicksteed and Lionel Robbins (the man who appointed

Hayek to the London School of Economics in 1931). Whereas William Stanley Jevons, the father of neoliberal economics, conceptualized labour as a form of *disutility* that centred on a *work/income trade-off* (i.e., people will put up with the displeasure of work until they reach the point where any extra income gained isn't worth it), a major shift occurs in later writers who speak of a *leisure/income trade-off* instead (i.e., people will forgo leisure time for an income, up until the point where it isn't worth it). As Derobert concludes, in the new worldview, 'labor is indeed absent . . . standing for the phantom of the model. Everywhere the concepts of leisure, income, and wage rate are displayed, while labor is overlooked. Even the wage is presented not as the price of work, but as the opportunity cost of leisure: L. Derobert, (2001). 'On the Genesis of the Canonical Labor Supply Model'. *Journal of the History of Economic Thought*, 23(2): 197–215, p. 199.

27   As James K. Galbraith argues in his critical reading of mainstream US economics, even the rudimentary notion of supply-and-demand, taught in most universities around the world, is predicated on the formal absence of a real workforce. If the supply curve theoretically represents someone's willingness (or unwillingness) to sell something at a certain price in relation to demand, then there can be no supply curve in a labour market since eating, supporting a family and paying the mortgage will prefigure any so-called 'choice' to work or not. J. K. Galbraith (2008). *The Predator State: How Conservatives Abandoned the Free Market and Why Liberals Should Too*. New York: Free Press, p. 154.

28   I. Gershon (2017). *Down and Out in the New Economy: How People Find (or Don't Find) Work Today*. University of Chicago Press.

29   M. Friedman and R. Friedman (1980). *Free to Choose: A Personal Statement*. San Diego: Harcourt.

30   A. Smith (2017). 'Deliveroo installs "dark kitchens" for customers ordering restaurant food'. *Metro*. Available at http://metro.co.uk/2017/10/29/deliveroo-installs-dark-kitchens-for-customers-ordering-restaurant-food-7036495.

31   P. Vigna and M. Casey (2016). *Cryptocurrency: How Bitcoin and*

Digital Money are Challenging the Global Economic Order. New York: Vintage.

32   As Hayek argued in a 1985 television interview: 'I am absolutely convinced that no government is capable of politically or intellectually proving the exact amount of money that is needed for smooth economic development. In fact I am convinced that we shall never have decent money again before we take from government the monopoly of issuing money and allow competing institutions . . . [and] competing monies and let people decide which they prefer to use': F. A. Hayek (1985). 'Hayek on Milton Friedman and Monetary Policy'. Interview available at https://www.you tube.com/watch?v=fXqc-yyoVKg&t=4s. It's also important to note that the Bitcoin speculative bubble of 2017–18 revealed that it's quite unlike real money: alt-currencies don't reference anything outside of themselves and thus have no relational value. As Kleiner points out in a fascinating essay, Bitcoin is technically worthless, symbolizing a 'fair price' of zero. See D. Kleiner (2018). 'Bitcoin: Proof of Work and the Labour Theory of Value'. *P2P Foundation*. Available at https://blog.p2pfoundation.net/face-value-bitcoin-proof-work-labourvalue/2018/02/01.

33   See P. Toynbee and D. Walker (2017). *Dismembered: How the Conservative Attack on the State Harms Us All*. London: Faber.

34   See M. Blyth (2013). *Austerity: The History of a Dangerous Idea*. New York: Oxford University Press.

35   For example, see J. Taplin (2017). *Move Fast and Break Things: How Facebook, Google, and Amazon Cornered Culture and Undermined Democracy*. Boston, MA: Little, Brown.

36   D. Graeber (2015). *Utopia of Rules: On Technology, Stupidity and the Secret Joys of Bureaucracy*. Brooklyn: Melville House.

37   It's interesting to note how Hayek's thought evolved on this question, which is an important ideological prelude to the more predatory state that dominates Western economies today. In *The Road to Serfdom*, he dismisses the state almost completely, whereas in 1960's *The Constitution of Liberty*, Hayek's tune changes slightly, perhaps registering the importance of some centralized body for propping up the so-called 'spontaneity' of the market order: 'it is

the character rather than the volume of government activity that is important' (p. 222).

38   See A. Azmanova (2010). 'Capitalism Reorganized: Social Justice after Neo-liberalism'. *Constellations*, 17(2): 390–406.

39   L. Truss (2018). 'The Conservative Case for Disruption'. *CAPX*. Available at https://capx.co/the-conservative-case-for-disruption.

40   Firms in the platform economy often attempt to temper this narrative of self-reliance by adding an element of charity. For example, Airbnb calls itself 'an economic lifeline' to lower socio-economic groups, providing 'a social safety net' in difficult times. See C. Hendrickson (2018). 'The Gig Economy's Great Delusion'. *The Boston Review*. Available at http://bostonreview.net/class-inequality/clara-hendrickson-gig-economys-great-delusion.

41   This individualistic version of 'freedom' goes to the heart of the neoliberal economic project, which is strictly anti-public in nature and oriented around personal cash exchange. For example, Hayek argues: 'freedom thus presupposes that the individual has some assured private sphere' (Hayek, *The Constitution of Liberty*, p. 61). For early Chicago University economist Frank Knight, this 'is simply the freedom of the individual to "deal" with any and all other individuals and to select the best terms as judged by himself, among those offered': F. Knight (1941). 'The Meaning of Freedom'. *Ethics*, 52(1): 86–109, 102.

Chapter One Uberfamiliar

1   P. Noor (2017). 'Sex for Rent? It's the Logical Extension of Leaving Housing to the Market.' *The Guardian*. Available at https://www.theguardian.com/commentisfree/2017/apr/19/sex-rent-logical-extension-leaving-housing-to-market.

2   S. Rea (2017). 'The Londoners Who Offer Free Rent for Sexual Favours'. *Londonist*. Available at http://londonist.com/2016/09/the-londoners-who-offer-free-rent-for-sexual-favours.

3   See M. Desmond (2017). *Evicted: Poverty and Profit in the*

American City. Penguin: New York; A. Minton (2017). *Big Capital: Who is London For?* London: Penguin.

4   See A. Verity and N. Stylianou (2018). 'Firms on Caribbean Island Chain Own 23,000 UK Properties'. *BBC News.* Available at www. bbc.co.uk/news/business-42666274.

5   R. Obordo (2016). '"I'm At the Mercy of my Landlord": Life as a Young Renter'. *The Guardian.* Available at https://www.the guardian.com/commentisfree/2016/jun/16/im-at-the-mercy-of-my-landlord-life-as-a-young-renter.

6   For example, see C. Taylor (2014). 'Plantation Neoliberalism'. *New Inquiry.* Available at https://thenewinquiry.com/plantation-neoliberalism.

7   R. Best (2009). 'Time to Regulate'. *The Future of the Private Rented Sector*, p. 68. Quoted in A. Minton (2009). *Ground Control: Fear and Happiness in the Twentieth-Century City.* London: Penguin, p. 111.

8   See R. Neuwirth (2011). *Stealth of Nations: The Global Rise of the Informal Economy.* New York: Anchor Books; N. Gilman, J. Goldhammer and S. Weber (2011). *Deviant Globalization: Black Market Economy in the 21st Century.* New York: Continuum.

9   C. C. Williams (2014). 'Out of the Shadows: A Classification of Economies by the Size and Character of their Informal Sector'. *Work, Employment and Society*, 28(5): 735–53.

10   N. Srnicek (2016). *Platform Capitalism.* Cambridge: Polity.

11   See F. A. Hayek (1944). *The Road to Serfdom.* London: Routledge; F. A. Hayek (1945). 'The Use of Knowledge in Society'. *American Economic Review*, 35(4): 519–30.

12   A. Amin (2012). *Land of Strangers.* Cambridge: Polity.

13   J. Kantor and D. Streitfeld (2015). 'Inside Amazon: Wrestling Big Ideas in a Bruising Workplace'. *The New York Times.* Available at www.nytimes.com/2015/08/16/technology/inside-amazon-wrestling-big-ideas-in-a-bruising-workplace.html?_r=0.

14   Ibid.

15   R. W. Jones (2016). 'Ex-Hermes Courier Says She Suffered the "Life from Hell" while Working for the Firm'. *The Mirror.* Available

at www.mirror.co.uk/news/uk-news/ex-hermes-courier-says-suffered-8660714.

16 Ibid.

17 See H. Hester and N. Srnicek (2018). *After Work: The Fight for Free Time*. London: Verso.

18 M. Weber (1946). *From Max Weber: Essays in Sociology*. New York: Oxford University Press.

19 See Hayek. *The Road to Serfdom*.

20 See P. Fleming (2009). *Authenticity and the Cultural Politics of Work*. Oxford University Press.

21 See P. Ranis (2016). *Cooperatives Confront Capitalism: Challenging the Neoliberal Economy*. London: Zed Books.

22 J. K. Galbraith (2008). *The Predatory State*. New York: Free Press, p. 19.

23 See, for example, M. Friedman and R. Friedman (1980). *Free to Choose: A Personal Statement*. San Diego: Harcourt.

24 For Frank Knight, free market capitalism is ethically superior to state control because it celebrates 'the freedom of the individual to "deal" with any and all other individuals and to select the best terms as judged by himself, among those offered': F. Knight (1941). 'The Meaning of Freedom'. *Ethics*, 52(1): 86–109, p. 102.

25 De Jasay significantly influenced Public Choice Theory (discussed in chapter 3) and its cynicism towards the state and public officials: 'my definition of the capitalist state requires it to opt for a sort of unilateral disarmament, for a self-denying ordinance concerning the property of its subjects and their freedom to negotiate contracts with each other': A. de Jasay (1985). *The State*. Indianapolis: The Liberty Fund, p. 32.

26 Galbraith, *The Predatory State*.

27 M. Lazzarato (2012). *The Making of Indebted Man: Essay on the Neoliberal Condition*. Los Angeles: Semiotexte.

28 Anonymous (2016a). 'No Phones, Low Pay, Sent Home for Purple Hair – Life on a Zero-hours Contract'. *The Guardian*. Available at https://www.theguardian.com/commentisfree/2016/jul/19/no-phones-low-pay-sent-home-purple-hair-life-zero-hours-contract.

29 It's unfortunate that mainstream jurisprudence continues to dominate scholarly analysis of contracts, even in this deformalized setting. More fruitful inquiry might be gained from other disciplines, including psychoanalysis and its cognates. For example, Gilles Deleuze's fascinating study of masochism could shed new light on contracts and agreements if analysed closely. In any power relationship, he argues, the law perpetually overrides a contract because its very structure demands more (submission) than is textually stated in the fine print. Documents always embody a *tactical excess* in this sense, which is really just the social setting in which the contract is articulated. Perhaps this is why so-called 'agreements' are now so popular, particularly in the gig economy, because they capture both the contractual and obligatory. They're excruciatingly open-ended, relying on a knowing 'nod-and-a-wink' among the participants in order to function. See G. Deleuze (2006). *Coldness and Cruelty*. New York: Zone Books, p. 92.

30 R. Epstein (2015). 'Richard Epstein Enriches Us with His Ideas on Inequality, Taxes, Politics, and Health Care'. *The Hoover Institution*. Available at https://www.youtube.com/watch?v=7sJPZeSl-5M.

31 R. Epstein (2001). 'Employment and Labor Law Reform in New Zealand Lecture'. *Journal of International Law* 33: 370.

32 Oxfam (2018). 'Reward Work, Not Wealth'. Available at https://policy-practice.oxfam.org.uk/publications/reward-work-not-wealth-to-end-the-inequality-crisis-we-must-build-an-economy-fo-620396.

33 UBS/PwC (2017). 'UBS/PwC Billionaires Report: New Value Creators Gain Momentum'. Available at https://www.ubs.com/microsites/billionaires-report/en/new-value.html.

34 R. Neat (2017). 'World's Witnessing a New Gilded Age as Billionaires' Wealth Swells to $6tn'. *The Guardian*. Available at https://www.theguardian.com/business/2017/oct/26/worlds-witnessing-a-new-gilded-age-as-billionaires-wealth-swells-to-6tn.

35 UBS/PwC. 'UBS/PwC Billionaires Report'.

36 N. Hopkins (2017). 'Tax Haven Lobby Boasted of "Superb Penetration" at Top of UK Government'. *The Guardian*. Available at https://www.theguardian.com/news/2017/nov/07/tax-haven-lobby-superb-penetration-uk-government-paradise-papers.

37 M. Nippert (2017). 'Citizen Thiel'. *New Zealand Herald*. Available at www.nzherald.co.nz/indepth/national/how-peter-thiel-got-new-zealand-citizenship.

38 M. O'Connell (2018). 'Why Silicon Valley Billionaires Are Prepping for the Apocalypse in New Zealand'. *The Guardian*. Available at https://www.theguardian.com/news/2018/feb/15/why-silicon-valley-billionaires-are-prepping-for-the-apocalypse-in-new-zealand.

39 Nippert. 'Citizen Thiel'.

40 B. Milanović (2016). *Global Inequality: A New Approach for the Age of Globalization*. Princeton University Press.

41 Ibid., p. 215.

42 For example, Hayek states: 'we shall indeed see that many of those who demand an extension of equality do not really demand equality but a distribution that conforms more closely to human conceptions of individual merit and that their desires are as irreconcilable with freedom as the more strictly egalitarian demands': Hayek (1960). *The Constitution of Liberty*. Chicago University Press, p. 150. Milton Friedman justified inequality in a similar vein, but took the argument one step further. For him, there's no difference between someone who inherits a fortune from their parents and a child who's born with innate singing talents. To interfere in either case in the name of 'equality' is ethically wrong: Friedman and Friedman. *Free to Choose*, p. 136. From a European perspective, Anthony de Jasay argues that sound and judicious statecraft is 'reluctant to promote the good of society, let alone to order the more fortunate of its subjects to share their good fortune with the less fortunate, not because it lacks compassion, but because it does not consider that having creditable and honourable feelings entitles the state to coerce its subjects into indulging them: De Jasay, *The State*, p. 35.

43 For example, see arguments forwarded by neoconservative US

jurist Richard Epstein: Epstein, 'Richard Epstein Enriches Us with His Ideas on Inequality, Taxes, Politics, and Health Care'.

44   Milanović. *Global Inequality.*

45   S. Goldberg (2013). 'College "Sugar Babies" Date for Cash'. *CNN.* Available at http://edition.cnn.com/2013/02/26/living/students-sugar-daddy-relationships/index.html.

Chapter Two Sugar Daddy Capitalism

1   B. Wade (2014). 'Dating Website Founder Says Love Doesn't Exist'. *CNN.* Available at http://edition.cnn.com/2014/09/25/opinion/seeking-arrangement-ceo-on-love.

2   J. Diaz and A. Valiente (2014). 'What It's Like to Go Out with Someone Who Bought Your Date Online'. *ABC News.* Available at http://abcnews.go.com/Lifestyle/bought-date-online/story?id=26839200; K. Trammel (2014). 'Student Shares Experiences as a Sugar Baby: Not All Gifts, Glamour'. *The Red and Black.* Available at www.redandblack.com/uganews/student-shares-experiences-as-a-sugar-baby-not-all-gifts/article_d862db14-28c1-11e4-97a8-001a4bcf6878.html.

3   J. Bauer-Wolf (2017). 'Students with Sugar Daddies'. *Inside Higher Ed.* Available at https://www.insidehighered.com/news/2017/04/17/students-and-sugar-daddies-age-student-debt.

4   J. Edwards (2014). 'This MIT Nerd Built A "Sugar Baby" Dating Empire that Some Say Is Simply Prostitution'. *Business Insider.* Available at www.businessinsider.com/brandon-wade-of-seekingarrangment-biography-2014-3?op=1&IR=T/#-mit-in-the-1990s-i-was-very-much-a-nerd-he-told-business-insider-2.

5   Ibid.

6   Wade, 'Dating Website Founder Says Love Doesn't Exist'.

7   Ibid.

8   R. Normandin (2011). 'The Dark Side of an MIT Brain'. *The Tech.* Available at http://tech.mit.edu/V131/N34/normandin.html.

9   J. Giuffo (2012). 'MissTravel.com: Dating Site or Travel Ho Dating Site?' *Forbes.* Available at https://www.forbes.com/sites/

johngiuffo/2012/04/27/misstravel-com-dating-site-or-travel-ho-dating-site/#306d6e8a5696.

10 S. Goldberg (2013). 'College "Sugar Babies" Date for Cash'. *CNN*. Available at http://edition.cnn.com/2013/02/26/living/students-sugar-daddy-relationships/index.html.

11 Ibid.

12 P. Judy (2013). 'True Story: We Were WhatsYourPrice Sugarbabies'. *Virginity Movies*. Available at https://www.virginitymovie.com/blog/2013/07/true-story-we-were-whatsyourprice-com-sugarbabies.

13 Ibid.

14 Ibid.

15 J. Bullen (2017). '"Men Think You're Their Pet": "Sugar Baby" Reveals Hidden Dangers Behind Earning £1,000-a-month for Sex and Dating'. *Daily Mirror*. Available at www.mirror.co.uk/news/uk-news/men-think-youre-pet-sugar-9919714.

16 A. Sundararajan (2016). *The Sharing Economy: The End of Employment and the Rise of Crowd-Based Capitalism*. Cambridge, MA: MIT Press.

17 F. A. Hayek (1944). *The Road to Serfdom*. London: Routledge.

18 As opposed to natural law and legal positivism, Hayek argues, 'from the fact that the rule of law is a limitation upon all legislation, it follows that it cannot itself be a law in the same sense as the laws passed by the legislator': F. A. Hayek (1960). *The Constitution of Liberty*. University of Chicago Press, p. 310.

19 Hayek, *The Road to Serfdom*, p. 44.

20 Ibid., p. 68.

21 Ibid., p. 72.

22 G. Becker (1974). 'A Theory of Marriage'. In T. Schultz (ed.), *Economics of the Family: Marriage, Children, and Human Capital*. Cambridge, MA: NBER Books, pp. 299–351.

23 J. Greenwood, N. Guner, G. Kocharkov and C. Santos (2014). 'Marry Your Like: Assortative Mating and Income Inequality'. *American Economic Review*, 104(5): 348–53.

24 Goldberg, 'College "Sugar Babies" Date for Cash'.

25 D. McDonald (2017). 'Harvard Business School and the

Propagation of Immoral Profit Strategies'. *Newsweek*. Available at www.newsweek.com/2017/04/14/harvard-business-school-financial-crisis-economics-578378.html.

26 Hayek, *The Road to Serfdom*, p. 56.
27 Ibid., p. 72. Also see Hayek's celebration of 'independent' workers who get paid on an individual basis for exactly what they do, as opposed to regular employees who are collectively paid for simply being a member of an organization: Hayek, *The Constitution of Liberty*, p. 188.
28 Bullen, '"Men Think You're Their Pet"'.
29 Anonymous (2016). 'No Phones, Low Pay, Sent Home for Purple Hair – Life on a Zero-Hours Contract'. *The Guardian*. Available at https://www.theguardian.com/commentisfree/2016/jul/19/no-phones-low-pay-sent-home-purple-hair-life-zero-hours-contract.
30 Hayek, *The Road to Serfdom*, p. 71.
31 See A. Ross (2014). *Creditocracy and the Case for Debt Refusal*. New York: Or Books.
32 Financial Stability Board (2017). 'Global Shadow Banking Monitoring Report 2016'. Available at www.fsb.org/2017/05/global-shadow-banking-monitoring-report-2016.
33 For example, see G. Zucman (2017). 'The Desperate Inequality Behind Global Tax Dodging'. *The Guardian*. Available at https://www.theguardian.com/commentisfree/2017/nov/08/tax-havens-dodging-theft-multinationals-avoiding-tax; also see R. Murphy (2017). *Dirty Secrets: How Tax Havens Destroy the Economy*. London: Verso.
34 Financial Global Integrity (2016). 'Trade Misinvoicing'. Available at www.gfintegrity.org/issue/trade-misinvoicing.
35 J. Bartlett (2014). *The Dark Net: Inside the Digital Underworld*. New York: Melville House.
36 Ibid, p. 3.
37 K. Marx (1988). *Economic and Philosophic Manuscripts of 1844*. New York: Prometheus Books, p. 138.
38 M. Friedman (1962). *Capitalism and Freedom*. University of Chicago Press.

39   Hayek, *The Road to Serfdom*, pp. 95–6.

40   M. Friedman (1980). *Free to Choose*, part 8: 'Who Protects the Worker?' Available at https://www.youtube.com/watch?v= Gb6aqitTgOM.

41   Ibid.

42   Ibid.

43   J. McMartin (2011). *Collision Course: Ronald Reagan, the Air Traffic Controllers, and the Strike that Changed America*. New York: Oxford University Press.

44   See M. Friedman (1994). 'Milton Friedman on Hayek's "Road to Serfdom" 1994 Interview'. Available at https://www.youtube. com/watch?v=15idnfuyqXs&t=715s.

45   See P. Fleming (2017). 'What is Human Capital?' *Aeon*. Available at https://aeon.co/essays/how-the-cold-war-led-the-cia-to-pro mote-human-capital-theory.

46   See M. Friedman (2010). 'Uncommon Knowledge: Milton Friedman on Libertarianism'. Available at https://www.youtube. com/watch?v=JSumJxQ5oy4&t=1093s.

47   R. Epstein (1978). 'Medical Malpractice: Its Cause and Cure'. In S. Rottenberg (ed.), *The Economics of Medical Malpractice*. Washington, DC: The American Enterprise Institute, p. 225.

48   E. Saner (2016). 'War on Wheels: An Uber Driver and a Black-Cab Driver Debate London's Taxi Trade'. *The Guardian*. Available at https://www.theguardian.com/technology/2016/feb/12/war-on-wheels-uber-driver-black-cab-driver-debate-london-taxi-trade.

49   A. Bish and A. Davidson (2016). 'Paedophile Hunters: Should Police Be Working with Vigilantes?' *BBC News*. Available at www. bbc.co.uk/news/magazine-37708233.

50   B. Malkin and G. Cleland (2007). 'Police Recruit 16-year-old Support Officers'. *The Telegraph*. Available at www. telegraph.co.uk/news/uknews/1560166/Police-recruit-16-year-old-support-officers.html.

51   M. Gove (2010). 'Oral Answers to Questions: Education'. House of Commons. Available at https://publications.parliament.uk/pa/ cm201011/cmhansrd/cm101115/debtext/101115-0001.htm.

52   M. Steel (2013). 'Of Course You Don't Need Qualified Teachers

in Free Schools. Or Qualified Brain Surgeons, for that Matter'. *The Independent.* Available at www.independent.co.uk/voices/comment/of-course-you-don-t-need-qualified-teachers-in-free-schools-or-qualified-brain-surgeons-for-that-8916236.html.

53　H. Mance (2016). 'Britain Has Had Enough of Experts, Says Gove'. *Financial Times.* Available at https://www.ft.com/content/3be49734-29cb-11e6-83e4-abc22d5d108c.

54　D. Carrington (2017). 'Green Movement "Greatest Threat to Freedom", Says Trump Adviser'. *The Guardian.* Available at https://www.theguardian.com/environment/2017/jan/30/green-movement-greatest-threat-freedom-says-trump-adviser-myron-ebell.

55　See T. Nichols (2017). *The Death of Expertise: The Campaign Against Established Knowledge and Why it Matters.* New York: Oxford University Press.

Chapter Three　Wiki-feudalism

1　L. Dearden (2017). 'Grenfell Tower Fire: Six-month-old Baby Found Dead in Mother's Arms in Stairwell, Inquest Hears'. *The Independent.* Available at www.independent.co.uk/news/uk/home-news/grenfell-tower-fire-baby-leena-belkadi-found-dead-mother-arms-stairwell-inquest-north-kensington-a78 13901.html.

2　It was later revealed that this council (dominated by the Conservative Party) actually enjoyed a budget surplus of £274m in 2014. K. Forster (2017). 'Grenfell Tower's Fireproof Cladding was "Downgraded to Save £293,000", Show Leaked Documents'. *The Independent.* Available at https://www.independent.co.uk/news/uk/home-news/grenfell-tower-cladding-fireproof-downgrade-save-money-cut-cost-293000-leak-documents-north-a7815971.html.

3　S. Knapton and H. Dixon (2017). 'Eight Failures that Left People of Grenfell Tower at Mercy of the Inferno'. *The Telegraph.* Available at www.telegraph.co.uk/news/2017/06/15/eight-failures-left-people-grenfell-tower-mercy-inferno.

4　M. Bulman (2017). 'Grenfell Tower Fire: Cladding Used on Block

"Was Banned in US"'. *The Independent*. Available at www.inde pendent.co.uk/news/uk/home-news/grenfell-tower-fire-latest-london-cladding-banned-us-flammable-a7792711.html.

5   Knapton and Dixon, 'Eight Failures'.

6   A. Hosken (2017). 'Fire Brigade Raised Fears about Cladding with Councils'. *BBC News*. Available at www.bbc.co.uk/news/uk-40422922.

7   C. York (2017). 'Grenfell Tower Refurbishment: Residents Warned Landlord KCTMO Building Was a Fire Risk'. *Huffington Post*. Available at www.huffingtonpost.co.uk/entry/grenfell-tower-fire_uk_5940d081e4b0d3185485cf62.

8   L. Pasha-Robinson (2017). 'Sadiq Khan Says '"Questions to be Answered" after Grenfell Tower Residents Told to Stay in Flats'. *The Independent*. Available at www.independent.co.uk/news/uk/home-news/london-fire-sadiq-khan-grenfell-tower-residents-mayor-stay-in-flats-dead-fatalities-north-kensington-a7788911.html.

9   Knapton and Dixon, 'Eight Failures'.

10 N. McIntyre (2017). 'England's Fire Services Suffer 39% Cut to Safety Officers Numbers'. *The Guardian*. Available at https://www.theguardian.com/uk-news/2017/aug/29/englands-fire-services-suffer-39-cut-to-safety-officers-numbers.

11 Ibid.

12 Parliament.uk (2014). '6 Feb 2014: "Brandon Lewis: Parliamentary Business"'. Available at https://publications.parliament.uk/pa/cm201314/cmhansrd/cm140206/halltext/140206h0002.htm.

13 T. Clark (2017). 'London Building Act "Would Have Averted Grenfell Disaster"'. *Construction News*. Available at www.constructionnews.co.uk/best-practice/health-and-safety/london-building-act-would-have-averted-grenfell-disaster/10020920.article.

14 Ibid.

15 G. Monbiot (2017). 'With Grenfell Tower, We've Seen What "Ripping Up Red Tape" Really looks Like'. *The Guardian*. https://www.theguardian.com/commentisfree/2017/jun/15/grenfell-tower-red-tape-safety-deregulation.

16   National Archives (2014). 'Red Tape Challenge: Prime Minister Announces Government Exceeds its Target to Identify 3,000 Regulations to be Amended or Scrapped'. Available at http://webarchive.nationalarchives.gov.uk/20150319091615/http://www.redtapechallenge.cabinetoffice.gov.uk/themehome/pm-speech-2; also see Gov.uk (2013). 'Red Tape Challenge is Removing Unnecessary Housing, Construction and Planning Regulations'. Available at https://www.gov.uk/government/news/red-tape-challenge-is-removing-unnecessary-housing-construction-and-planning-regulations.

17   Ibid.

18   W. Wainwright (2014). 'What Cameron's Bonfire of the Building Regulations Will Do to Our Homes'. *The Guardian*. Available at https://www.theguardian.com/artanddesign/architecture-design-blog/2014/jan/27/david-cameron-bonfire-of-building-regulations-future-homes.

19   S. Poole (2017). '"Deadlier than Terrorism": the Right's Fatal Obsession with Red Tape'. *The Guardian*. Available at https://www.theguardian.com/politics/2017/jun/20/deadlier-than-terrorism-right-fatal-obsession-red-tape-deregulation-grenfell-tower.

20   Gov.uk (2011). 'PM's Speech on Big Society'. Available at https://www.gov.uk/government/speeches/pms-speech-on-big-society.

21   G. Wilkes (2015). 'Steve Hilton: the Tory Guru Out of Step with Political Realities'. *Financial Times*. Available at https://www.ft.com/content/94ba1a62-ffcb-11e4-bc30-00144feabdc0.

22   G. Parker and J. Pickard (2011). 'Hilton Wants to Abolish Maternity Leave'. *Financial Times*. Available at https://www.ft.com/content/11cc97ae-b85f-11e0-b62b-00144feabdc0.

23   Ibid.

24   S. Hilton (2015). *More Human: Designing a World Where People Come First*. New York: W. H. Allen.

25   S. Teles (2010). *The Rise of the Conservative Legal Movement: The Battle for Control of the Law*. Princeton University Press. Also see J. Stiglitz (2017). 'America Has a Monopoly Problem – and It's

Huge'. *The Nation*. Available at https://www.thenation.com/arti
cle/america-has-a-monopoly-problem-and-its-huge.

26 Founding Chicago School economist Frank Knight argued, 'It is
needful to state that the role of "monopoly" in actual economic
life is enormously exaggerated in the popular mind and also that a
large part of the monopoly which is real, and especially the worst
part, is due to the activities of government': F. Knight (1941). 'The
Meaning of Freedom.' *Ethics* 52(1): 86–109, p. 103. The point is
later restated by Knight: 'the public has most exaggerated ideas
of the scope of monopoly as really bad and irremediable, and talk
of "abolishing" it is merely ignorant or irresponsible. There is no
clear line between legitimate and necessary profit and the monopoly gain that presents a problem for action': F. Knight (1953).
'Conflict of Values: Freedom and Justice'. In Alfred Dudley Ward
(ed.), *Goals of Economic Life*. New York: Harper and Brothers,
pp. 224–5.

27 See J. Weissmann (2018). 'Why Is It So Hard for Americans to Get
a Decent Raise?' *Slate*. Available at https://slate.com/business/
2018/01/a-new-theory-for-why-americans-cant-get-a-raise.
html; D. H. Autor, D. Dorn, L. F. Katz, C. Patterson and J. Van
Reenen (2017). 'Concentrating on the Fall of the Labor Share'.
CESifo Working Paper Series No. 6336. Available at SSRN: https://
ssrn.com/abstract=2932777.

28 Hilton, *More Human*, p. 39.

29 Ibid., p. 47.

30 Ibid., p. 163.

31 *BBC News* (2010). 'Cameron Aide Steve Hilton Arrested at Station
in 2008'. Available at http://news.bbc.co.uk/1/hi/uk_politics/
8447239.stm.

32 Parker and Pickard, 'Hilton Wants to Abolish Maternity Leave'.

33 P. L. Winter, R. B. Cialdini, R. J. Bator, K. Rhoads and B. J. Sagarin
(1998). 'An Analysis of Normative Messages in Signs at Recreation
Settings'. *Journal of Interpretation Research*, 3(1): 39–47.

34 Hilton, *More Human*, p. 122.

35 Ibid., pp. 102–3.

36 Ibid., pp. xxiv–xxv.

37 See S. Harney (2009). 'Extreme Neo-liberalism: An Introduction'. *Ephemera*, 9(4): 318–29.

38 N. Gilman, J. Goldhammer and S. Weber (2011). *Deviant Globalization: Black Market Economy in the 21st Century*. New York: Continuum.

39 A. Chandler (1977). *The Visible Hand: The Managerial Revolution in American Business*. Cambridge, MA: Harvard University Press.

40 M. Weber (1946). *From Max Weber: Essays in Sociology*. New York: Oxford University Press.

41 A. Gouldner (1954). *Patterns of Industrial Bureaucracy*. New York: Free Press; C. Wright Mills (1951). *White Collar: The American Middle Classes*. New York: Oxford University Press

42 H. Marcuse (1964). *One-Dimensional Man: Studies in the Ideology of Advanced Industrial Society*. New York: Beacon Press.

43 Ibid., p. 1.

44 I. Illich (1971). *Deschooling Society*. New York: Harper & Row.

45 I. Illich (1973). *Tools for Conviviality*. London: Calder Boyars, p. xii.

46 F. A. Hayek (1944). *The Road to Serfdom*. London: Routledge, p. 67.

47 F. A. Hayek (1945). 'The Use of Knowledge in Society'. *American Economic Review*, 35(4): 519–30, p. 526.

48 See J. Buchanan (1975*). Limits of Liberty: Between Anarchy and Leviathan*. University of Chicago Press; J. Buchanan and G. Tullock (1962/1990). *The Calculus of Consent: Logical Foundations of Constitutional Democracy*. Ann Arbor: University of Michigan; W. Niskanen (1996). *Bureaucracy and Public Economics*. Cheltenham: Edward Elgar Publishing Ltd.

49 *Frontier Centre* (1986). 'Conversations with Professor James M. Buchanan, Nobel Prize Laureate in Economics.' Available at www.iedm.org/files/011025buchananinterview.pdf.

50 R. Michels (1915/1962). *Political Parties: A Sociological Study of the Oligarchical Tendencies of Modern Democracy*. New York: Free Press.

51 See P. Toynbee and D. Walker (2017). *Dismembered: How the Conservative Attack on the State Harms Us All*. London: Faber.

52 P. Butler (2017). 'Council Spending on "Neighbourhood" Services Falls by £3bn since 2011'. *The Guardian*. Available at https://www. theguardian.com/society/2017/apr/25/spending-on-council-services-in-england-fell-3bn-in-past-five-years-study-bin-collec tions-local-government.

53 T. Crewe (2016). 'The Strange Death of Municipal England'. *London Review of Books*. Available at https://www.lrb.co.uk/v38/ n24/tom-crewe/the-strange-death-of-municipal-england.

54 McIntyre, 'England's Fire Services Suffer 39% Cut to Safety Officers Numbers'.

55 R. Evans (2016). '"Health Risk" Warning over Fall in Food Safety Checks'. *BBC News*. Available at www.bbc.co.uk/news/ uk-36171891. Also see Toynbee and Walker, *Dismembered*.

56 Evans, '"Health Risk" Warning over Fall in Food Safety Checks'.

57 Centre for Crime and Justice Studies (2016). 'Social Murder Kills Thousands Each Year'. Available at https://www.crimeandjustice. org.uk/news/social-murder-kills-thousands-each-year.

58 J. Doward (2016). 'Unchecked Pollution and Bad Food "Killing Thousands in UK"'. *The Guardian*. Available at https://www. theguardian.com/environment/2016/apr/30/pollution-food-poisoning-health-safety-deaths-thinktank.

59 A. Wasley (2018). '"Dirty Meat": Shocking Hygiene Failings Discovered in US Pig and Chicken Plants'. *The Guardian*. Available from https://www.theguardian.com/animals-farmed/2018/feb/ 21/dirty-meat-shocking-hygiene-failings-discovered-in-us-pig-and-chicken-plants.

60 Centers for Disease Control and Prevention (2017). 'Foodborne Illnesses and Germs'. Available at https://www.cdc.gov/food-safety/foodborne-germs.html.

61 A. Hill (2017). 'Home Office Makes Thousands in Profit on Some Visa Applications'. *The Guardian*. Available at https://www. theguardian.com/uk-news/2017/sep/01/home-office-makes-800-profit-on-some-visa-applications https://www.cdc.gov/food safety/foodborne-germs.html.

62 Ibid.

63 Ibid.

64 M. Reynolds (2016). 'Morale of UK Border Force Workers at "Rock Bottom" with One in Five Wanting to QUIT'. *Express*. Available at https://www.express.co.uk/news/uk/735193/UK-Border-Force-workers-morale-low-leaked-survey.

65 P. S. Adler and B. Borys (1996). 'Two Types of Bureaucracy: Enabling and Coercive'. *Administrative Science Quarterly*, 41: 61–89.

66 See C. B. Tansel (2016). *States of Discipline: Authoritarian Neoliberalism and the Contested Reproduction of Capitalist Order*. London: Rowman & Littlefield; P. Bloom (2016). *Authoritarian Capitalism in the Age of Globalization*. London: Edward Elgar.

67 Weber, *From Max Weber*; also see C. Perrow (2002). *Organizing America: Wealth, Power and the Origins of American Capitalism*. Princeton University Press.

68 Weber, *From Max Weber*, p. 224.

69 Ibid.

70 R. Edwards (1979). *Contested Terrain: The Transformation of the Workplace in the Twentieth Century*. New York: Basic Books.

71 Ibid., p, 162.

72 For example, see B. Watson (1971). 'Counter-planning on the Shopfloor'. *Radical America*, 5: 77–85.

Chapter Four The Human . . . All–Too–Human Workplace

1 F. Laloux (2014). *Reinventing Organizations: A Guide to Creating Organizations Inspired by the Next Stage in Human Consciousness*. Brussels: Nelson Parker.

2 R. Hodge (2015). 'First, Let's Get Rid of All the Bosses'. *New Republic*. Available at https://newrepublic.com/article/122965/can-billion-dollar-corporation-zappos-be-self-organized.

3 F. Laloux (2017). 'It's Time to Reinvent Organizations'. Available at www.reinventingorganizations.com.

4 Hodge, 'First, Let's Get Rid of All the Bosses'.

5 B. Robertson (2016). *Holacracy: The Revolutionary Management System that Abolishes Hierarchy*. New York: Portfolio Penguin.

6   A. Groth (2015). 'Holacracy at Zappos: It's Either the Future of Management or a Social Experiment Gone Awry'. *Quartz*. Available at https://qz.com/317918/holacracy-at-zappos-its-either-the-future-of-management-or-a-social-experiment-gone-awry.

7   Ibid.

8   Robertson, *Holacracy*.

9   J. Reingold (2016). 'How a Radical Shift Left Zappos Reeling'. *Fortune*. Available at http://fortune.com/zappos-tony-hsieh-holacracy.

10 Groth, 'Holacracy at Zappos'.

11 B. Lam (2016). 'Why Are So Many Zappos Employees Leaving?' *The Atlantic*. Available at https://www.theatlantic.com/business/archive/2016/01/zappos-holacracy-hierarchy/424173.

12 A. Groth (2015). 'Internal Memo: Zappos is Offering Severance to Employees Who Aren't All In with Holacracy'. *Quartz*. Available at https://qz.com/370616/internal-memo-zappos-is-offering-severance-to-employees-who-arent-all-in-with-holacracy.

13 B. Taylor (2008). 'Why Zappos Pays New Employees to Quit – And You Should Too'. *Harvard Business Review*. Available at https://hbr.org/2008/05/why-zappos-pays-new-employees.

14 B. Synder (2015). '14% of Zappos' Staff Left after Being Offered Exit Pay'. *Fortune*. Available at http://fortune.com/2015/05/08/zappos-quit-employees.

15 Reingold, 'How a Radical Shift Left Zappos Reeling'.

16 Lam, 'Why Are So Many Zappos Employees Leaving?'

17 Reingold, 'How a Radical Shift Left Zappos Reeling'.

18 Groth, 'Holacracy at Zappos'.

19 Ibid.

20 Reingold, 'How a Radical Shift Left Zappos Reeling'.

21 See T. Peters (1992). *Liberation Management: Necessary Disorganization for the Nanosecond Nineties*. New York: Alfred A. Knopf; T. Hsieh (2010); *Delivering Happiness: A Path to Profits, Passion and Purpose*. New York: Business Plus.

22 Peters, *Liberation Management*.

23 See L. Boltanski and E. Chiapello (2006). *The New Spirit of Capitalism*. London: Verso.

24 S. Hilton (2015). *More Human: Designing a World Where People Come First*. New York: W. H. Allen.

25 See P. Fleming (2015). *The Mythology of Work: How Capitalism Persists Despite Itself*. London: Pluto Press.

26 See L. French (2016). 'Zappos' Weird Management Style Is Costing It More Employees'. *Time*. Available at http://time.com/4180791/zappos-holacracy-buyouts.

27 For example, see C. DesMarais (2012). 'Your Employees Like Hierarchy (No, Really)' Inc. Available at https://www.inc.com/christina-desmarais/your-employees-like-hierarchy-no-really.html.

28 E. Zimmerman (2014). 'Jeffrey Pfeffer: Do Workplace Hierarchies Still Matter?' Insights from Stanford Business. Available at https://www.gsb.stanford.edu/insights/jeffrey-pfeffer-do-workplace-hierarchies-still-matter.

29 J. Peterson (2018). 'Jordan Peterson Talks Lobster on Channel 4 16th January 2018'. Available at https://www.youtube.com/watch?v=bZnygvRRmPE.

30 See M. Pick (2017). 'Cut the Bullshit: Organizations with No Hierarchy Don't Exist'. *Medium*. Available at https://medium.com/ouishare-connecting-the-collaborative-economy/cut-the-bullshit-organizations-with-no-hierarchy-dont-exist-f0a845e73a80.

31 Hilton, *More Human*, p. 208.

32 I. Trump (2010). *Trump Card: Playing to Win in Life and Work*. New York: Touchstone Books.

33 Ibid., p. 100.

34 Australian Broadcasting Corporation (2016). 'The Bullying and Hazing Inside Australia's Most Humiliating Workplace'. Available at www.news.com.au/finance/work/at-work/the-bullying-and-hazing-inside-australias-most-humiliating-workplace/news-story/012886ca98839ecc6cb8a11eca370e02.

35 Ibid.

36 L. Knowles and E. Worthington (2016). 'Appco: Workers Allegedly Forced to "Shove Cigarettes Up Bottoms" After Missing Sales Targets'. ABC. Available at www.abc.net.au/news/2016-11-05/

fresh-allegations-of-bizarre-rituals-at-marketing-giant-appco/
7996710.

37 L. Knowles (2017). 'Appco Class Action: Video Emerges Showing
Sales Team Being Forced to Simulate Sex Acts with Colleagues'.
ABC. Available at www.abc.net.au/news/2017-02-14/video-
shows-appco-workers-forced-simulate-sex-acts-class-action/
8268848.

38 See T. W. Adorno and M. Horkheimer (1947/2002). *The Dialectic
of the Enlightenment*. Stanford University Press. According to
them, de Sade conclusively reveals what the capitalist enlightenment movement cannot face about itself, how humanity
might be 'rationalized even in its breathing spaces' (p. 69),
allowing economic hatred to enter the realm of practical reason
(p. 87).

39 B. Ginsberg (2011). *The Fall of the Faculty: The Rise of the All-
Administrative University and Why It Matters*. New York: Oxford
University Press.

40 *Times Higher Education* (2014). 'Imperial College London to
"Review Procedures" after Death of Academic'. Available at
https://www.timeshighereducation.com/news/imperial-college-
london-to-review-procedures-after-death-of-academic/2017188.
article.

41 D. Colquhoun (2014). 'Publish *and* Perish at Imperial College
London: the Death of Stefan Grimm'. DC's Impossible Science
Blog. Available at www.dcscience.net/2014/12/01/publish-and-
perish-at-imperial-college-london-the-death-of-stefan-grimm.

42 Ibid.

43 J. Grove (2015). 'Stefan Grimm Inquest: New Policies May Not
Have Prevented Suicide'. *Times Higher Education*. Available at
https://www.timeshighereducation.com/news/stefan-grimm-
inquest-new-policies-may-not-have-prevented-suicide/2019563.
article.

44 During private moments, academics in the UK embarrassingly
admit to 'playing the game' when it comes to getting ahead, and
navigating this curious couplet of metrics and intimidation. In
his fascinating book *Mediocracy*, Alain Deneault argues that this

'game' is very similar to the one played by criminal gang members, as depicted in the TV show *The Wire*: 'the game is a euphemism for another political order: one that is badly structured, that cannot be spoke of even by those who maintain it year in and year out, and that is arbitrary, unpredictable and, of course, resolutely undemocratic . . . formal rules – laws, regulations, protocols – may continue to exist, of course, but they're destined to either be broken or instrumentalized'. In this regard, I don't think it's a coincidence that F. A. Hayek and Milton Friedman liked referring to the 'rule of law' (the bare legal minimum) as 'rules of the game': A. Deneault (2018). *Mediocracy: The Politics of the Extreme Centre*. Toronto: Between The Lines, p. 34.

45 Ron Srigley makes a perceptive argument on this topic when discussing the rise of the all-administrative university. A major reversal has taken place in the power structure. Professors of yesteryear were once considered unaccountable and senior administrators totally accountable. Now the opposite is the case. Srigley asks a poignant question: what exactly is the mandate of this new university? 'The administrators are the mandate . . . administrators are free to govern the university in whatever way they see fit so long as the mandate is furthered. If this requires some rough play to get the job done, so be it. If it requires, say, serially violating collective agreements to assert dominance and set precedent . . . so be it.'

Srigley argues that metrics and bullying go hand-in-hand in this setting. He shares an incident in which a professor he knew wrote to faculty colleagues raising concerns about a proposed performance measurement system. The new policy was sponsored by the Vice President and was met with little resistance, since most 'were petrified of losing their positions'. Some time later, the Vice President called a meeting with the professor and said (in Srigley's words): 'he was naïve to think his university email account was not "transparent" to his "managers." No discussion, no context, no actual accusation, and no reprimand. Just a thinly veiled threat that if he didn't watch out he'd find himself at the bottom of the academic East River . . . He learned subsequently that his email account hadn't been compromised at all; he'd simply been betrayed by a fellow-traveling faculty member. Which means the president was just having a little fun threatening him.' R. Srigley (2018). 'Whose University is it Anyway?' *Los Angeles Review of Books.* Available at https://lareviewofbooks.org/article/whose-university-is-it-anyway/#_edn1.

46 C. Parr (20). 'Imperial College Professor Stefan Grimm "Was Given Grant Income Target"'. *Times Higher Education.* Available at https://www.timeshighereducation.com/news/imperial-col lege-professor-stefan-grimm-was-given-grant-income-target/ 2017369.article.

47 Imperial College London (2015). 'Professor Alice Gast on BBC Radio 4's *Today Programme* (Friday, 17 April 2015)'. Available at https://wwwf.imperial.ac.uk/imedia/content/view/4708/prof essor-alice-gast-on-bbc-radio-4s-today-programme-friday-17-april-2015.

48 H. Simon (1991). 'Organisations and Markets'. *Journal of Economic Perspectives,* 5(2): 225–44, p. 237.

49 A. Avegoustaki (2016). 'Work Uncertainty and the Extensive Work Effort: the Mediating Role of Human Resource Practices'. *International Labor Review,* 69(3): 656–82.

50 K. Marx (1867/1976). *Capital: Volume One.* London: Penguin.

51 Ibid., p. 271.

52 Ibid.

53 A. Malm (2015). *Fossil Capital: The Rise of Steam Power and the Roots of Global Warming.* London: Verso.

54 Ibid., p. 130.

55 Groth, 'Holacracy at Zappos'.

56 J. Stanford (2017). 'The Resurgence of Gig Work: Historical and Theoretical Perspectives'. *Economic and Labour Relations Review* 28(3): 382–401.

57 Ibid. p. 386.

58 Ibid.

59 T. Brass (2004). 'Medieval Working Practices? British Agriculture and the Return of the Gangmaster'. *Journal of Peasant Studies* 31(2): 313–40.

60 See A. Hill (2017). 'Gig Workers Are Easy Prey for Bullies and Gangmasters'. *Financial Times.* Available at https://www.ft.com/content/cae35762-b41d-11e7-aa26-bb002965bce8?emailId=59e891ac60feaa0004330e63; P. Conford and J. Burchardt (2011). 'The Return of the Gangmaster'. *History and Policy*, 6 September. Available at www.historyandpolicy.org/policy-papers/papers/the-return-of-the-gangmaster.

61 A. Boyle (2018). 'Amazon Wins a Pair of Patents for Wireless Wristbands that Track Warehouse Workers'. *GeekWire.* Available at https://www.geekwire.com/2018/amazon-wins-patents-wireless-wristbands-track-warehouse-workers.

62 N. Schreiber (2017). 'How Uber Uses Psychological tricks to Push Drivers' Buttons'. *The New York Times.* Available at https://www.nytimes.com/interactive/2017/04/02/technology/uber-drivers-psychological-tricks.html?mtrref=www.google.co.uk&gwh=90ABE34EFF5B5EDEC703C24A8FACF16F&gwt=pay.

63 O. Solon (2017). 'Big Brother Isn't Just Watching: Workplace Surveillance Can Track Your Every Move'. *The Guardian.* Available at https://www.theguardian.com/world/2017/nov/06/workplace-surveillance-big-brother-technology.

64 Ibid.

65 G. Harvey, C. Rhodes, S. J. Vachhani and K. Williams (2017). 'Neo-villeiny and the Service Sector: the Case of Hyper Flexible and Precarious Work in Fitness Centres'. *Work, Employment and Society* 31(1): 19–35.

66 Ibid., p. 20.

67 See M. Weber, (1946). *From Max Weber: Essays in Sociology.* New York: Oxford University Press.

68 Harvey et al., 'Neo-villeiny and the Service Sector', p. 26.

69 Ibid., p. 30.

70 W. Streeck (2016). *How Will Capitalism End?* London: Verso.

71 D. Gordon (2017). 'Do You Have to Avoid Huggers at Work?' *BBC News.* Available at http://www.bbc.co.uk/news/business-40580986.

72 A. Swales (2016). 'The Rules of Digital Kissing: Is It Ever Appropriate to Sign off Work Emails with a Kiss?' *Stylist.* Available at www.

stylist.co.uk/life/rules-of-digital-kissing-email-kiss-etiquette-at-work-careers-workplace.

73 O. Williams-Grut (2014). 'Booze Trolleys and Cocktails in the Foyer: Why Londoners Are All Drinking al Desko'. *Evening Standard*. Available at https://www.standard.co.uk/lifestyle/foodanddrink/booze-trolleys-and-cocktails-in-the-foyer-why-londoners-are-all-drinking-al-desko-9581096.html.

74 G. Deleuze (1992). 'Postscript on the Societies of Control'. *October* 59(Winter): 3–7, p. 6.

75 For example, one survey of 1,000 employees regarding office Christmas parties found that 54 per cent will try to avoid them: *Reward Gateway* (2015). 'More than 50% of Employees Dread the Christmas Office Party'. Available at https://www.rewardgateway.com/press-releases/50-employees-dread-office-christmas-party.

76 Hart Research Associates (2016). 'Key Findings from a Survey of Women Fast Food Workers'. Available at http://hartresearch.com/wp-content/uploads/2016/10/Fast-Food-Worker-Survey-Memo-10-5-16.pdf.

77 Ibid., p. 2.

78 Ibid., p. 1.

79 See, for example, L. Dodson (2009). *The Moral Underground: How Ordinary Americans Subvert an Unfair Economy*. New York: The New Press.

80 F. A. Hayek (1944). *The Road to Serfdom*. London: Routledge.

81 A. Arendt (1958). *The Human Condition*. University of Chicago Press.

Chapter Five No More Buddy Buddy

1 M. Judge (dir.) (1999). *Office Space*. Twentieth Century Fox.

2 A 2017 poll of 5,000 UK workers found that 67 per cent were planning an 'exit route' from their present jobs. See R. Rigby (2017). 'Is the UK Workforce a Zombie Nation?' TotalJobs.com. Available at https://www.totaljobs.com/insidejob/uk-workforce-zombie-nation.

3   C. B. Macpherson (1962). *The Political Theory of Possessive Individualism: From Hobbes to Locke*. Toronto: Oxford University Press, Canada, p. 3.

4   Other victories in the UK alone are noteworthy in this regard – including e-commerce firm UK Express (UKXD), which admitted its couriers were employees in January 2018 after pressure from labour union GMB, and settled out of court; a case taken by three drivers for the taxi firm Addison Lee found in favour of the workers, stating that they were in fact employees; a 2018 court win for a cycle courier with CitySprint, which ruled that she was entitled to paid holiday leave and the national minimum wage.

5   Employment Appeal Tribunal (2017). '*Uber B.V. and Others* v. *Mr Y. Aslam and Others*'. Available at https://assets.publishing.service.gov.uk/media/5a046b06e5274a0ee5a1f171/Uber_B.V._and_Others_v_Mr_Y_Aslam_and_Others_UKEAT_0056_17_DA.pdf.

6   A. Rosenblat and L. Stark (2016). 'Algorithmic Labor and Information Asymmetries: A Case Study of Uber's Drivers'. *International Journal of Communication*, 10: 3758–84, p. 3762.

7   J. Worland (2017). 'Uber Wants to Settle a Lawsuit With its California Drivers for Just $1 Each'. *Fortune*. Available at http://fortune.com/2017/02/02/uber-california-lawsuit-settlement.

8   D. Alba (2016). 'Judge Rejects Uber's 100 Million Settlement with Drivers'. *Wired*. Available at https://www.wired.com/2016/08/uber-settlement-rejected.

9   United States District Court (2016). 'Order Denying Plaintiff's Motion for Preliminary Settlement'. Available at https://assets.documentcloud.org/documents/3031645/Uber-Settlement-Denied.pdf.

10 T. Lien (2015). 'Uber Tries to Limit Size in Class-Action Lawsuit with New Driver Contract'. *LA Times*. Available at www.latimes.com/business/technology/la-fi-tn-uber-arbitration-opt-out-20151211-story.html.

11 Uber Technologies, Inc. (2015). 'Technologies Services Agreement'. Available at https://s3.amazonaws.com/uber-regulatory-documents/country/united_states/RASIER+Technology+Services+Agreement+December+10+2015.pdf.

12 Ibid.

13 Lien, 'Uber Tries to Limit Size in Class-Action Lawsuit with New Driver Contract'.

14 Ibid.

15 S. Fowler (2017). 'Reflecting on One Very, Very Strange Year at Uber'. Available at https://www.susanjfowler.com/blog/2017/2/19/reflecting-on-one-very-strange-year-at-uber.

16 Ibid.

17 Ibid.

18 P. Blumberg (2017). 'Ex-Uber Engineer Asks Supreme Court to Learn from Her Ordeal'. Bloomberg. Available at https://www.bloomberg.com/news/articles/2017-08-24/uber-provocateur-takes-her-tale-of-harassment-to-supreme-court.

19 N. Tiku (2017). 'Why Aren't More Employees Suing Uber?' *Wired*. Available at https://www.wired.com/story/uber-susan-fowler-travis-kalanick-arbitration.

20 M. Hamilton (2017). 'Labor Protections Rise in New York's Uber, Lyft Debate'. *Times Union*. Available at www.timesunion.com/tuplus-local/article/Labor-protections-rise-in-New-York-s-Uber-Lyft-10842682.php.

21 J. Woodcock (2016). 'Lessons on Resistance from Deliveroo and UberEATS'. Pluto Press Blog. Available at https://www.plutobooks.com/blog/lessons-on-resistance-from-deliveroo-and-ubereats.

22 Ibid.

23 S. Butler and H. Osbourne (2016). 'Deliveroo Announces It Will Not Force New Contracts on Workers'. *The Guardian*. Available at https://www.theguardian.com/business/2016/aug/16/deliveroo-announces-it-will-not-force-new-contracts-on-workers.

24 Woodcock, 'Lessons on Resistance from Deliveroo and Uber EATS'.

25 J. Woodcock (2016). 'Slaveroo: Deliveroo Drivers Organising in the "Gig Economy"'. *Novara Media*. Available at http://novaramedia.com/2016/08/12/slaveroo-deliveroo-drivers-organising-in-the-gig-economy.

26 *Fortune* (2017). 'Ryanair Recognizes Pilot Union in Historic Effort

to Stop Holiday Season Strike'. Available at http://fortune.com/2017/12/15/ryanair-strike-pilot-union-recognize.

27 D. Morris (2017). 'Uber Names New Self-Driving Car Hardware Chief Amid Major Turmoil'. *Fortune*. Available at http://fortune.com/2017/06/09/uber-new-head-of-self-driving-hardware-development.

28 J. Woodcock (2016). *Working the Phones: Control and Resistance in a Call Centre*. London: Pluto Press.

29 Ironically, these rather subjective judgement calls are increasingly being conducted by AI in the recruitment process, with companies like Hirevue pioneering software that uses cameras and algorithms to measure posture, facial expressions and vocal tone in job interviews. See S. Buranyi (2018). 'Dehumanising, Impenetrable, Frustrating: the Grim Reality of Job Hunting in the Age of AI'. *The Guardian*. Available at https://www.theguardian.com/inequality/2018/mar/04/dehumanising-impenetrable-frustrating-the-grim-reality-of-job-hunting-in-the-age-of-ai.

30 G. Callaghan and P. Thompson (2002). '"We Recruit Attitude": the Selection and Shaping of Routine Call-Centre Labour'. *Journal of Management Studies*, 39(2): 233–54.

31 Ibid., p. 240.

32 R. Brooks (2012). *Cheaper by the Hour: Temporary Lawyers and the Deprofessionalization of the Law*. Philadelphia: Temple University Press.

33 Ibid., p. 130.

34 Ibid., p. 135.

35 Ibid., p. 140.

36 R. Tracey (2015). 'Driverless Trains Would Break the Militant Unions Forever'. *City AM*. Available at www.cityam.com/222879/tube-strike-driverless-trains-would-break-militant-unions-forever; T. Edwards (2011). 'Driverless Tube Trains: Is This the End for Drivers?' *BBC News*. Available at www.bbc.co.uk/news/uk-england-london-15523336.

37 For example, see G. Monbiot (2017). *Out of the Wreckage: A New Politics for an Age of Crisis*. London: Verso; P. Fleming (2017). *The Death of Homo Economicus*. London: Pluto Press.

38   C. Lispector (1977). *The Hour of the Star*. São Paulo: Jose Olympio, p. 15.

39   M. Weaver (2017). 'G4S Staff Suspended from Brook House Immigration Centre over Abuse Claims'. *The Guardian*. Available at https://www.theguardian.com/uk-news/2017/sep/01/g4s-staff-suspended-brook-house-immigration-centre-claims-abuse.

40   Ibid.

41   R. Epstein (2014). 'The Moral and Economic Foundations of Capitalism'. The Clemson Institute. Available at https://www.youtube.com/watch?v=5gwKh3C4f_Q.

42   R. Epstein (2016). 'Richard Epstein's Lecture on Piketty'. Available at https://www.youtube.com/watch?v=B2NYie_EAL4&t=463s.

43   F. Phillips (2017). 'The Gig Economy: Using Mandatory Arbitration Agreements with Class Action Waivers'. *Lexology*. Available at https://www.lexology.com/library/detail.aspx?g=93b55903-50ac-49a6-9663-67b23acc9f08.

44   D. Alba (2016). 'Judge Says Lyft's $12 Million Settlement Doesn't Pay Drivers Enough'. *Wired*. Available at https://www.wired.com/2016/04/judge-says-lyfts-12m-settlement-doesnt-pay-drivers-enough.

45   H. Somerville (2016). 'Judge Approves $27 Million Driver Settlement in Lyft Lawsuit'. Reuters. Available at https://www.reuters.com/article/us-lyft-drivers/judge-approves-27-million-driver-settlement-in-lyft-lawsuit-idUSKBN16N30D.

46   D. Levine and H. Somerville (2016). 'Lyft Settles California Driver Lawsuit over Employment Status'. Reuters. Available at https://www.reuters.com/article/us-lyft-drivers-settlement/lyft-settles-california-driver-lawsuit-over-employment-status-idUSKCN0V-50FR.

47   *BBC News* (2017). 'Deliveroo Claims Victory in Self-Employment Case'. Available at www.bbc.co.uk/news/business-41983343.

48   Ibid.

49   L. Crampton and J. Steingart (2017). 'Uber, Lyft Court Filing Marks New Justice Dept. Initiative'. Bloomberg. Available at https://www.bna.com/uber-lyft-court-n73014471763.

50   Section 6 of the Clayton Act of 1914 states that 'The labor of a

human being is not an article of commerce and that nothing contained in the antitrust laws shall be construed to forbid the existence and operation of labor . . . organizations, instituted for the purposes of mutual help, . . .or to forbid or restrain individual members of such organizations from lawfully carrying out the legitimate objects thereof; nor shall such organizations, or the members thereof, be held or construed to be illegal combinations or conspiracies in restraint of trade, under the antitrust laws'. Available at http://gwclc.com/Library/America/USA/The%20 Clayton%20Act.pdf.

51 See H. Simons (1942). 'Hansen on Fiscal Policy.' *Journal of Political Economy*, 50: 171; H. Simons (1944). 'Some Reflections on Syndicalism'. *Journal of Political Economy*, 52: 1–25; Fritz Machlup (1947). 'Monopolistic Wage Determination as a Part of the General Problem of Monopoly'. In *The Economic Institution on Wage Determination and Economics of Liberalism*. Washington, DC: The Chamber of Economics of the United States, pp. 49–82; F. A. Hayek (1960). *The Constitution of Liberty*. University of Chicago Press, p. 391.

52 F. Knight (1953). 'Conflict of Values: Freedom and Justice'. In Alfred Dudley Ward (ed.), *Goals of Economic Life*. New York: Harper and Brothers, pp. 224–5.

53 B. Jessop (2003). *The Future of the Capitalist State*. Cambridge: Polity.

54 *BBC News* (2016). 'French Workers Get "Right to Disconnect" from Emails out of Hours'. Available at www.bbc.co.uk/news/ world-europe-38479439.

55 J. Appleton (2016). *Officious: Rise of the Busybody State*. London: Zero Books; B. Evans and S. McBride (2017). *The Austerity State*. University of Toronto Press.

56 F. A. Hayek (1944). *The Road to Serfdom*. London: Routledge.

57 M. Weber (1946). *From Max Weber: Essays in Sociology*. New York: Oxford University Press, p. 226.

58 R. Michels (1915/1962). *Political Parties: A Sociological Study of the Oligarchical Tendencies of Modern Democracy*. New York: Free Press.

59 See W. Niskanen (1996). *Bureaucracy and Public Economics.* Cheltenham: Edward Elgar Publishing Ltd.

60 A. Sen. (1977). 'Rational Fools: A Critique of the Behavioral Foundations of Economic Theory'. *Philosophy and Public Affairs,* 6(4): 317–44.

61 C. Sellers (2017). 'Trump and Pruitt are the Biggest Threat to the EPA in its 47 Years of Existence'. *Vox.* Available at https://www. vox.com/2017/7/1/15886420/pruitt-threat-epa.

62 M. Mazzucato (2013). *The Entrepreneurial State: Debunking Public vs. Private Sector Myths.* London: Anthem Press.

63 D.Graeber (2015). *The Utopia of Rules: On Technology, Stupidity and the Secret Joys of Bureaucracy.* Brooklyn: Melville House.

64 Modern Monetary Theory offers interesting insights here. For example, see W. Mitchell and T. Fazi (2017). *Reclaiming the State: A Progressive Vision of Sovereignty for a Post-Neoliberal World.* London: Pluto Press; W. Mosler (2010). *Seven Deadly Innocent Frauds of Economic Policy.* St Croix: Valance.

65 See M. Blyth (2013). *Austerity: The History of a Dangerous Idea.* New York: Oxford University Press; A. Pettifor (2017). *The Production of Money: How to Break the Power of Bankers.* London: Verso.

66 Hayek argues, for example, that 'freedom thus presupposes that the individual has some assured private sphere': Hayek, *The Constitution of Liberty,* p. 61.

Conclusion *Less* Human

1 Hayek explicitly argues neoclassical political economists must learn from the socialists and their capacity for deep utopian thinking: 'We must make the building of a free society once more an intellectual adventure, a deed of courage. What we lack is a liberal Utopia, a program which seems neither a mere defense of things as they are nor a diluted kind of socialism, but a truly liberal radicalism which does not spare the susceptibilities of the mighty (including the trade unions), which is not too severely practical, and which does not confine itself to what appears today

as politically possible. We need intellectual leaders who are willing to work for an ideal, however small may be the prospects of its early realization. They must be men who are willing to stick to principles and to fight for their full realization, however remote': F. A. Hayek (1949). 'The Intellectuals and Socialism'. *University of Chicago Law Review*, 16(3): 417–33, pp. 432–3.

2   C. Bray (2016). 'No Laptop, No Phone, No Desk: UBS Reinvents the Work Space'. *The New York Times*. Available at https://www. nytimes.com/2016/11/04/business/dealbook/ubs-bank-virtual-desktops-london.html?action.

3   Ibid.

4   Ibid.

5   F. A. Hayek (1944). *The Road to Serfdom*. London: Routledge.

6   R. Booth (2018). 'DPD Courier Who Was Fined for Day Off to See Doctor Dies from Diabetes'. *The Guardian*. Available at https:// www.theguardian.com/business/2018/feb/05/courier-who-was-fined-for-day-off-to-see-doctor-dies-from-diabetes.

7   S. Hilton (2015). *More Human: Designing a World Where People Come First*. New York: W. H. Allen.

8   Ibid., p. 163.

9   D. Pink (2014). *To Sell Is Human: The Surprising Truth about Moving Others*. London: Canongate Books Ltd.

10   Ibid., p. 6.

11   D. Pink (2013). 'Why "To Sell Is Human"'. Knowledge at Wharton. Available at https://www.youtube.com/watch?v=J6EjBwrdHgE& t=381s.

12   See A. Culp (2016). *Dark Deleuze*. Minneapolis: Minnesota University Press.

13   That's why there is no 'way of the wolf', as argued by Jordan Belford (of *Wolf of Wall Street* fame) in his recent book on how to become a killer salesperson. See J. Belford (2017). *Way of the Wolf: Straight Line Selling: Master the Art of Persuasion, Influence and Success*. New York: North Star Way.

14   G. Deleuze (2006). *Coldness and Cruelty*. New York: Zone Books.

15   G. Deleuze (2011). *Gilles Deleuze from A to Z*. Cambridge, MA: MIT Press.

16 N. Chomsky and M. Foucault (2006). *The Chomsky–Foucault Debate: On Human Nature.* New York: The Free Press.

17 See N. Chomsky (2017). *Optimism over Despair.* London: Penguin; N. Chomsky (2015). 'Noam Chomsky on Moral Relativism and Michel Foucault'. Available at https://www.youtube.com/watch?v=i63_kAw3WmE.

18 D. Harvey (2014). *Seventeen Contradictions and the End of Capitalism.* London: Profile Books.

19 Ibid., p. 287.

20 See T. Morton (2017). *Humankind: Solidarity with Nonhuman People.* London: Verso.

21 For more on this, see G. Standing (2017). *Basic Income: And How We Can Make It Happen.* London: Pelican/Penguin; R. Bregman (2016). *Utopia for Realists: The Case for a Universal Basic Income, Open Borders, and a 15-hour Workweek.* Amsterdam: The Correspondent.

22 For example, see E. A. Roy (2016). 'Zero-hours Contracts Banned in New Zealand'. *The Guardian.* Available at www.theguardian.com/world/2016/mar/11/zero-hour-contracts-banned-in-new-zealand.

23 A number of recent cases are notable: McDonald's workers going on strike in the UK for the first time; US fast-food workers opposing the industry's use of surprise scheduling; and immigrant night cleaners taking on a multinational sourcing firm in London and winning. See J. Kollewe and N. Slawson, (2017). 'McDonald's Workers to Go on Strike in Britain for First Time'. *The Guardian.* Available at https://www.theguardian.com/business/2017/sep/04/mcdonalds-workers-strike-cambridge-crayford; P. Szekely (2017). 'Not So Fast: US Restaurant Workers Seeking a Ban on Surprise Scheduling'. Reuters. Available at www.reuters.com/article/us-usa-fastfood-schedules/not-so-fast-u-s-restaurant-workers-seek-ban-on-surprise-scheduling-idUSKBN1A20VC; A. Chakrabortty (2017). 'College Cleaners Defeated Outsourcing: They've Shown It Can Be Done'. *The Guardian.* Available at https://www.theguardian.com/commentisfree/2017/sep/12/college-cleaners-outsourcing-soas.

24 See P. Fleming (2017). *The Death of Homo Economicus: Work, Debt and the Myth of Endless Accumulation*. London: Pluto.

25 A. Kleinknecht, Z. Kwee and L. Budyanto (2016). 'Rigidities through Flexibility: Flexible Labour and the Rise of Management Bureaucracies'. *Cambridge Journal of Economics*, 40(4): 1137–47, p. 1137.

26 L. Mishel and J. Schieder (2017). 'CEO pay remains high relative to the pay of typical workers and high-wage earners'. Economic Policy Institute. Available at http://www.epi.org/publication/ ceo-pay-remains-high-relative-to-the-pay-of-typical-workers- and-high-wage-earners/

27 It is interesting to note that Hayek made a concerted effort to poison the idea of worker co-operatives in the minds of both employers *and employees*. He saw them not only as a grave threat to capitalism, but illogical and stupid. While his argumentation borders on comedy, it did provide ammunition to neoliberal policy-makers and spokespeople when they were attacking a system that is often more productive, democratic and fulfilling: 'A plant or industry cannot be conducted in the interest of some permanent distinct body of workers if it is at the same time to serve the interests of the consumers. Moreover, effective participation in the direction of an enterprise is a full-time job, and anybody so engaged soon ceases to have the outlook and interest of an employee. It is not only from the point of view of the employers, therefore, that such a plan should be rejected; there are very good reasons why in the United States union leaders have emphatically refused to assume any responsibility in the conduct of business': F. A. Hayek (1960). *The Constitution of Liberty*. University of Chicago Press, p. 396.

28 For example, see A. Pang (2016). *Rest: Why You Get More Done When You Work Less*. New York: Penguin; H. Matharu (2016). 'Employers in Sweden Introduce Six-Hour Work Day'. *The Independent*. Available at www.independent.co.uk/news/world/ europe/sweden-introduces-six-hour-work-day-a6674646.html; P. Fleming (2015). *The Mythology of Work: How Capitalism Persists Despite Itself*. London: Pluto.

29 R. Epstein (2015). 'Richard Epstein Enriches Us with His Ideas

on Inequality, Taxes, Politics, and Health Care'. The Hoover Institution. Available at https://www.youtube.com/watch?v= 7sJPZeSl-5M.

30 In his unconvincing defence of at-will contracts, Epstein mentions in passing the criticism that workers may be dismissed due to their 'refusal to grant personal or sexual favours'. However, Epstein still sees them as preferable over one-size-fits-all state regulation (including just cause provisions), since the personal autonomy and freedom of both employer and employee ought to be sacrosanct. Once again, work is considered a completely private matter, a question of personal choice and preference. It's this ideology that is so perversely exploited under Sugar Daddy Capitalism: R. Epstein. (1984) 'In Defense of the Contract at Will'. *University of Chicago Law Review*, 51(4): 947–82, p. 949.

Index

Note: Page numbers with italic *f* indicate figures.

working in bar that uses insecure
contracts 50
see also Gatwick Airport; Imperial
College London; Parliament
(UK); Transport for London
London Building Act (1939/97)
63
London Fire Brigade 62
London Review of Books 173n(53)
London School of Economics
157n(26)
Los Angeles Review of Books 179n(45)
Lyft 10, 11, 125, 183n(20),
185nn(44–6/49)
rating system used by 101
see also Uber Lyft Teamsters

machine learning 125
Machlup, Fritz 133, 186n(51)
Macpherson, B. 182n(3)
Malkin, B. 167n(50)
Malm, Andreas 103, 179nn(53–4)
Mance, H. 168n(53)
Marcuse, Herbert 75, 172nn(42–3)
market individualism 3, 24f, 25, 26,
81, 92, 104, 140, 150, 151
attempt to overlay monetary
formalism of 71
cold 96
deformalization in relation to 4
monetarized 76
roadmap metaphor used to justify
112
society based on 129
Trojan Horse for privatizing social
influence 135
utopian image of 57
marketization 14
mass 155n(21)
Marling, B. 154n(8)
Marquis de Sade 96–7
Marx, Karl 53–4, 101–3, 131,
166n(37), 179n(50)
Marxism 92
radical 75
Massachusetts 120
Matharu, H. 190n(28)
Mazzucato, M. 187n(62)

McDonald, D. 165n(25)
McDonald's 189n(23)
McIntyre, N. 169n(10), 173n(54)
McMartin, J. 167n(43)
Mercier, Hugo 6, 155n(16)
Michels, Robert 77, 137, 172n(50),
186n(58)
micro-fascism 117, 119, 139
Microsoft 11
Milanović, Branko 33, 163nn(40–1),
164n(44)
Mises, Ludwig von 13, 154n(14)
Mishel, L. 190n(26)
MissTravel.com 37, 40, 44, 164–5n(9)
Mitchell, W. 187n(64)
Modern Monetary Theory 187n(64)
Monbiot, G. 169n(15), 184n(37)
Mondragon co-operative 25
Monero 12
monetary policy 3, 12
money 14, 19–20, 21
anonymity of 23, 49
blurring of life and 9
borrowing 51
chance to save 16
divine power of 53–4
extracting more from the
community 138
family 33
impartiality of 27
judgement of 15
liberty/freedom and 4, 42, 76
life is only about 43
nameless flows of 47
owners of 102
private economy 25
sleazy qualities of 50
society based on imperium of 129
Sugar Babies in it for 36, 38–9
symbiosis between selfhood and
143
worry about 7
young women meet older men
for 9
see also alt-currencies; cash
money creation 138
see also quantitative easing
money laundering 52